# pocket
# guide
# to

# SHOTGUNS
## identification and values

## 1900
## to
## present

Russell Quertermous

Steve Quertermous

The current values in this book should be used only as guide. They are not intended to set prices, which vary from one section of the country to another. Auction prices as well as dealer prices vary greatly and are affected by condition as well as demand. Neither the Author nor the Publisher assumes responsibility for any losses that might be incurred as a result of consulting this guide.

*Seaching for a Publisher?*
We are always looking for knowledgeable people considered experts within their fields. If you feel there is a real need for a book on your collectible subject and have a large comprehensive collection, contact us.

COLLECTOR BOOKS
P.O. Box 3009
Paducah, Kentucky 42002-3009

# Introduction

This is an identification and value guide. Very little in the way of instruction and directions should be required to use a value guide but some words of explanation might be in order.

First of all the suggested values are just that. They are not the final word on an item's absolute worth. That figure can only be determined by the buyer's willingness to purchase and the seller's ability to hold to an asking price. But the values found in this book should be a reasonable guide of what certain firearms are selling for on average around the country.

Geography plays an important part in establishing value. Some guns are more in demand in particular locales than other firearms that are equal in rarity, workmanship and quantities. There are also guns that have a good resale value just because they are manufactured by a particular company. Maybe the company's track record for producing high quality firearms is especially good. Or, maybe there is just an aura of greatness that has been associated with the manufacturer for one reason or another.

Condition is also important in establishing a value. The values in this guide relate to firearms in very good to excellent condidion. That is: in good working condition with no appreciable wear on working surfaces, no corrosion or pitting with only minor surface dents or scratches at one end of the spectrum to: in new condition, used very little, with no noticeable marring of the wood or metal and with perfect bluing except at the muzzle or on sharp edges.

The value range should be a reasonable guide to the gun's real selling worth. But readers who disagree with the pricing structure are encouraged to do further research to ascertain what they consider to be the value.

The illustrations in this guide are from gun companies' promotional materials and as such are not meant to be representative of size relation.

There is no way that a book of this size can be all inclusive of the firearms made in the world but we hope it is a good survey of most of the firearms that are readily available on the open market.

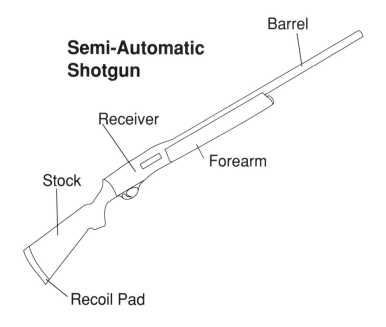

**Semi-Automatic Shotgun**

Barrel

Receiver

Forearm

Stock

Recoil Pad

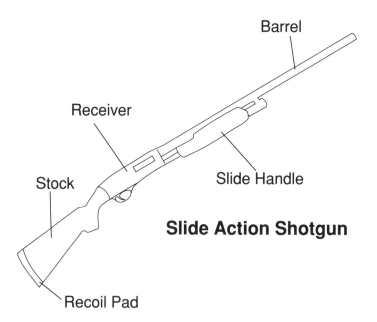

Barrel

Receiver

Slide Handle

Stock

**Slide Action Shotgun**

Recoil Pad

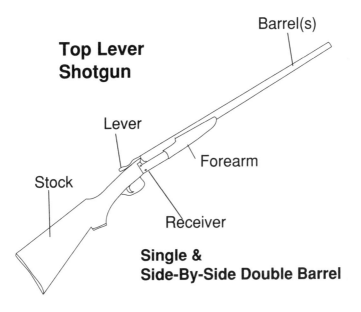

**Top Lever Shotgun**

Barrel(s)

Lever

Forearm

Stock

Receiver

**Single & Side-By-Side Double Barrel**

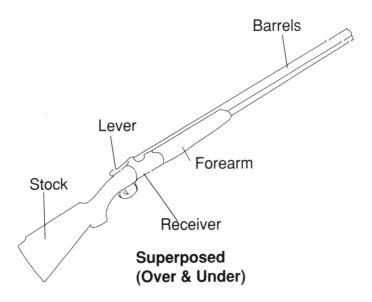

Barrels

Lever

Forearm

Stock

Receiver

**Superposed (Over & Under)**

# *Acknowledgments*

The companies included for the use of catalogs, advertisements and promotional material.

A special thanks to the following gun manufacturers for additional photos, information and assistance: Beretta Arms Co., Inc., Browning, Commercial Trading Imports, Inc. for material on Baikal shotguns, Harrington & Richardson, Inc., Ithaca Gun Co., Mannlicher, Marlin for material on Marlin and Marlin-Glenfield, O.F. Mossberg & Sons, Inc. for material on Mossberg and New Haven shotguns, Remington, Richland Arms Co., Savage Arms for material on Savage shotguns, Stevens shotguns, and Fox shotguns, Sears, Roebuck & Co., for material on Sears shotguns and Ted Williams shotguns; Smith & Wesson, Weatherby, Inc., Winchester-Western for material on Winchester shotguns, and U.S. Repeating Arms for material on Winchester shotguns.

Petersen Publishing Company for the use of photographs from *Guns and Ammo Annual*, 1977, 1982 and *Hunting Annual* 1983.

Russell Scheffer of Scheffer Studio for graphic arrangement of the material. Russell is always there, day or night, to crank out an amazing amount of work on extremely short notice.

The crew that makes up the editorial staff of Collector Books. Their dedication and hard work make an unbelievable number of books on antiques and collectibles indispensible tools for collectors everywhere.

# Contents

# AYA

**AYA Matador**
**Gauge:** 10, 12, 16, 20, 20 magnum
**Action:** Box lock; top lever break-open; hammerless; selective single trigger & automatic ejector
**Magazine:** None
**Barrel:** Double barrel, 26", 28", or 30" any choke combination
**Finish:** Blued; checkered walnut pistol grip stock & beavertail forearm
**Estimated Value: $360.00 - $450.00**

**AYA Matador II**
Same as the Matador except: ventilated rib
**Estimated Value: $400.00 - $500.00**

**AYA Bolero**
Same as the Matador except: non-selective single trigger & extractors; 28 & 410 gauges
**Estimated Value: $310.00 - $390.00**

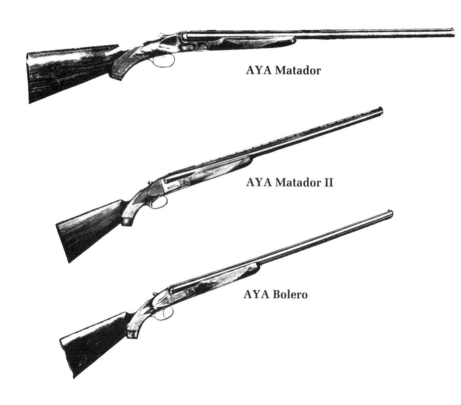

AYA Matador

AYA Matador II

AYA Bolero

# Armalite

**Armalite AR-17**

**Armalite AR-17**
**Gauge:** 12
**Action:** Semi-automatic; gas operated; hammerless
**Magazine:** 2-shot
**Barrel:** 24" aluminum alloy; interchangeable choke tubes
**Finish:** Gold anodized or black anodized; plastic stock & forearm
**Estimated Value: $500.00 - $675.00**

# Baikal

**Baikal Model IJK-27 and IJK-27EIC**
**Gauge:** 12 or 20
**Action:** Box lock; top lever break-open; hammerless; selective single trigger; IJK-27EIC has selective ejectors, add $40.00 for IJK-27EIC
**Magazine:** None
**Barrel:** Over & under double barrel; 26", 28", or 30" improved cylinder & modified or modified & full chokes; ventilated rib
**Finish:** Blued; engraved receiver; hand checkered walnut pistol grip stock & forearm
**Estimated Value: $240.00 - $300.00**

**Baikal Model IJK-27EIC Silver**
Same as the Model IJK-27EIC except: silver inlays and fancy engraving
**Estimated Value: $395.00 - $495.00**

**Baikal Model IJK-12**
Similar to the IJK-27 except: no engraving; no recoil pad; 28" barrel only
**Estimated Value: $200.00 - $250.00**

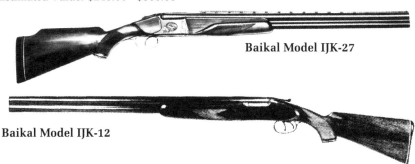

**Baikal Model IJK-27**

**Baikal Model IJK-12**

# Baikal

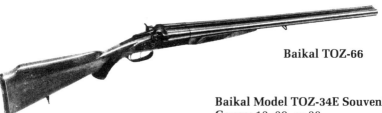

**Baikal TOZ-66**

**Baikal TOZ-66**
**Gauge:** 12
**Action:** Box lock; top lever break-open; exposed hammers
**Magazine:** None
**Barrel:** Double barrel (side by side); 28" chrome lined barrels; variety of chokes
**Finish:** Blued; checkered wood pistol grip stock & short tapered forearm; engraving
**Estimated Value: $205.00 - $260.00**

**Baikal Model TOZ-34E Souvenir**
**Gauge:** 12, 20, or 28
**Action:** Box lock; top lever break-open; hammerless; selective ejectors and cocking indicators
**Magazine:** None
**Barrel:** Over and under double barrel; 26" or 28" improved cylinder & modified or modified & full; ventilated rib on 12 and 20 gauge; solid rib on 28 gauge
**Finish:** Blued; select walnut, hand checkered pistol grip stock and forearm; engraved receiver
**Estimated Value: $450.00 - $600.00**

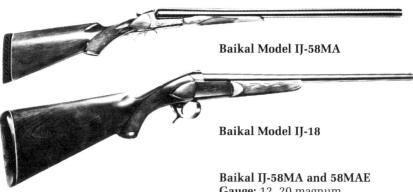

**Baikal Model IJ-58MA**

**Baikal Model IJ-18**

**Baikal Model IJ-18**
**Gauge:** 12, or 20
**Action:** Box lock; top lever break-open; hammerless; single shot; cocking indicator
**Magazine:** None
**Barrel:** 26", 28" modified, or 30" full choke
**Finish:** Blued; checkered walnut-stained hardwood pistol grip stock and tapered forearm; engraved receiver
**Estimated Value: $60.00 - $70.00**

**Baikal IJ-58MA and 58MAE**
**Gauge:** 12, 20 magnum
**Action:** Box lock; top lever break-open; hammerless
**Magazine:** None
**Barrel:** Double barrel (side by side); 26" improved cylinder & modified; 28" modified & full chokes; chrome lined
**Finish:** Blued; checkered walnut pistol grip stock and short tapered forearm; engraved receiver; IJ-58MAE has selective ejectors; add $28.00 for IJ-58MAE
**Estimated Value: $220.00 - $275.00**

**Baikal Model MC-8**
**Gauge:** 12
**Action:** Box lock; top lever break-open; hammerless
**Magazine:** None
**Barrel:** Over and under double barrel; trap, skeet; 26" or 28" modified or full chokes; chrome lined barrels
**Finish:** Blued; checkered walnut Monte Carlo pistol grip stock and forearm; engraved receiver
**Estimated Value: $1,300.00 - $1,800.00**

**Baikal Model MC-21**
**Gauge:** 12
**Action:** Semi-auto; hammerless; side ejection
**Magazine:** 5-shot tubular
**Barrel:** 26" improved cylinder; 28" modified; 30" full chokes; ventilated rib
**Finish:** Blued; checkered walnut pistol grip stock and forearm; engraved receiver
**Estimated Value: $250.00 - $325.00**

Baikal Model MC-21

Baikal Model MC-5

**Baikal Model MC-5**
**Gauge:** 20
**Action:** Box lock; top lever break-open; hammerless; double triggers
**Magazine:** None
**Barrel:** Over and under double barrel; 26" or 28" improved cylinder & modified or skeet chokes; ribbed
**Finish:** Blued; checkered walnut pistol grip or straight stock and forearm; engraved receiver
**Estimated Value: $650.00 - $850.00**

# Baker

**Baker Batavia Leader**

**Baker Black Beauty Special**
Similar to Baker Batavia Leader except: higher quality wood and finish; engraved; add $75.00 for automatic extractors
**Estimated Value: $500.00 - $675.00**

**Baker Black Beauty Special**

**Baker Batavia Leader**
**Gauge:** 12, 16, or 20
**Action:** Box lock; top lever break-0pen; hammerless; add $75.00 for automatic extractors
**Magazine:** None
**Barrel:** 26", 28", 30", or 32" double barrel (side by side); any standard choke combination
**Finish:** Blued; walnut pistol grip stock and forearm.
**Estimated Value: $360.00 - $450.00**

# Beretta

**Beretta Companion FS-1**

**Beretta Companion FS-1**
**Gauge:** 12, 16, 20, 28, or 410
**Action:** Underlever break-open; hammerless; single shot; folding shot gun
**Magazine:** None
**Barrel:** 26" or 28" full choke
**Finish:** Blued; checkered walnut pistol grip stock and forearm
**Estimated Value: $100.00 - $130.00**

**Beretta Model 412**
**Gauge:** 12, 20, 28, or 410
**Action:** Underlever, break-open; hammerless; single shot
**Magazine:** None
**Barrel:** 28" full or modified choke
**Finish:** Blued; checkered walnut semi-pistol grip stock and forearm
**Estimated Value: $130.00 - $160.00**

## Beretta Mark II Trap
**Gauge:** 12
**Action:** Box lock; top lever break-open; hammerless; single shot
**Magazine:** None
**Barrel:** 32" or 34" full choke; ventilated rib
**Finish:** Blued; checkered walnut Monte Carlo pistol grip stock and forearm; recoil pad; engraving
**Estimated Value: $420.00 - $525.00**

**Beretta Mark II Trap**

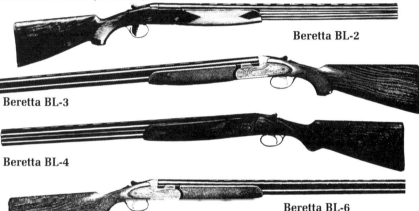

**Beretta BL-2**

**Beretta BL-3**

**Beretta BL-4**

**Beretta BL-6**

## Beretta BL-1
**Gauge:** 12
**Action:** Box lock; top lever break-open; hammerless; double triggers
**Magazine:** None
**Barrel:** Over and under double barrel; chrome steel; 26" or 30" improved cylinder & modified or modified & full chokes
**Finish:** Blued; checkered walnut semi-pistol grip stock and forearm
**Estimated Value: $365.00 - $460.00**

## Beretta BL-2
Similar to the BL-1 except: selective single trigger
**Estimated Value: $415.00 - $520.00**

## Beretta BL-3
Similar to the BL-2 except: ventilated rib; engraving
**Estimated Value: $520.00 - $650.00**

## Beretta BL-4 and BL-5
Similar to the BL-3 except: deluxe engraving and checkering; automatic ejectors; add $200.00 for BL-5
**Estimated Value: $600.00 - $750.00**

## Beretta BL-6
The finest of the BL line; highest quality checkering and engraving; automatic ejectors
**Estimated Value: $1,050.00 - $1,300.00**

# Beretta

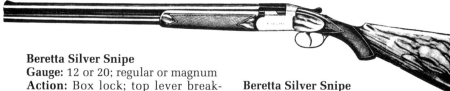

## Beretta Silver Snipe
**Gauge:** 12 or 20; regular or magnum
**Action:** Box lock; top lever break-open; hammerless; add $25.00 for single selective trigger
**Magazine:** None
**Barrel:** 26"or 30"; ribbed; over and under double barrel; improved cylinder & modified; modified & full; full or skeet chokes
**Finish:** Blued; nickel receiver; checkered walnut pistol grip stock and forearm
**Estimated Value: $440.00 - $550.00**

## Beretta Golden Snipe
Similar to the Silver Snipe except: ventilated rib; automatic ejectors
**Estimated Value: $560.00 - $700.00**

**Beretta Silver Snipe**

## Beretta Asel
**Gauge:** 12 or 20
**Action:** Box lock; top lever break-open; hammerless; automatic ejectors; single trigger
**Magazine:** None
**Barrel:** Over and under double barrel; 25", 28", or 30" improved cylinder & modified or modified & full chokes
**Finish:** Blued; checkered walnut semi-pistol grip stock and forearm
**Estimated Value: $1,050.00 - $1,325.00**

**Beretta Model S56E**

## Beretta Model S56E
Similar to Model S55B except; scroll engraving on the receiver; selective automatic ejectors
**Estimated Value: $640.00 - $800.00**

## Beretta Model S55B
**Gauge:** 12 or 20; regular or magnum
**Action:** Box lock; top lever break-open; hammerless
**Magazine:** None
**Barrel:** Over and under double barrel; chrome lined; ventilated rib; 26" improved cylinder & modified; 28" or 30" modified & full; 30" full in 12 gauge
**Finish:** Blued; checkered walnut pistol grip stock and beavertail forearm; recoil pad on magnum
**Estimated Value: $570.00 - $710.00**

**Beretta Model 680 Trap**

## Beretta Model 680 Competition Skeet
**Gauge:** 12
**Action:** Top lever, break-open; hammerless; automatic ejectors; single selective trigger
**Magazine:** None
**Barrel:** Over and under double barrel; 26" or 28" skeet choke barrels; ventilated rib
**Finish:** Blued; checkered walnut pistol grip stock and forearm; silver gray receiver with engraving; goldplated trigger
**Estimated Value: $1,050.00 - $1,320.00**

## Beretta Model 680 Trap
Similar to the Model 680 Skeet except: Monte Carlo stock recoil pad; 30" or 32" improved modified & full choke barrels
**Estimated Value: $1,060.00 - $1,330.00**

## Beretta Model 680 Mono Trap
Similar to the Model 680 Trap except: single barrel with a high ventilated rib; 32" or 34" full choke barrel
**Estimated Value: $1,075.00 - $1,340.00**

**Beretta Model 685**

## Beretta Model 625
**Gauge:** 12 or 20; regular or magnum
**Action:** Box lock; top lever break-open; hammerless
**Magazine:** None
**Barrel:** 26" improved cylinder & modified; 28" or 30" modified & full; double barrel (side by side)
**Finish:** Blued; gray receiver; checkered walnut pistol grip or straight stock and tapered forearm
**Estimated Value: $660.00 - $825.00**

## Beretta Model 626; 626 Onyx
Similar to the Model 625 except: selective automatic ejectors; deduct 30% for Model 626
**Estimated Value: $1,125.00 - $1,400.00**

## Beretta Model 627EL, 627EELL
Similar to the Model 626 except: higher grade finish and engraved sideplate; add 70% for EELL Model
**Estimated Value: $1,960.00 - $2,450.00**

## Beretta Model 685
**Gauge:** 12 or 20; regular or magnum
**Action:** Top lever, break-open; hammerless; single selective trigger
**Magazine:** None
**Barrel:** Over and under double barrel; 26" improved cylinder & modified, 28" or 30" modified & full, 30" full & full; ventilated rib
**Finish:** Blued; checkered walnut pistol grip stock and fluted forearm; silver gray receiver with light engraving
**Estimated Value: $620.00 - $775.00**

Beretta Model 687EELL

### Beretta Model 686
**Gauge:** 12 or 20; regular or magnum
**Action:** Top lever, break-open; hammerless; single selective trigger; selective automatic ejectors
**Magazine:** None
**Barrel:** Over and under double barrel; 26" improved cylinder & modified; 28" or 30" modified & full; 30" full & full; ventilated rib; multi-choke tubes available
**Finish:** Blued; checkered walnut pistol grip stock and fluted forearm; silver gray receiver with engraving; recoil pad on magnum; add 12% for Ultralight Onyx model; add 44% for Sporting Clays model
**Estimated Value:** $820.00 - $1,020.00

### Beretta Model 687L
**Gauge:** 12 or 20; regular or magnum
**Action:** Top lever, break-open; hammerless; selective automatic ejectors; single selective trigger
**Magazine:** None
**Barrel:** Over and under double barrel; 26" or 28" with interchangeable choke tubes; ventilated rib
**Finish:** Blued; grayed receiver with engraving; checkered walnut pistol grip stock and forearm; add 25% for Golden Onyx model; add 38% for Sporting Clays model
**Estimated Value:** $945.00 - $1,180.00

### Beretta Model 687EL, 687 EELL
Similar to the Model 687L except: higher quality finish, extensive engraving on receiver and sideplates; add 50% for EELL Model
**Estimated Value:** $1,910.00 - $2,385.00

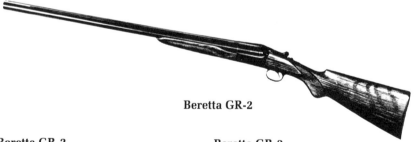

Beretta GR-2

### Beretta GR-2
**Gauge:** 12 or 20
**Action:** Box lock, top lever, break-open; hammerless
**Magazine:** None
**Barrel:** Double barrel (side by side); 26" or 30"; variety of choke combinations
**Finish:** Blued; checkered walnut semi-pistol grip stock and forearm
**Estimated Value:** $450.00 - $570.00

### Beretta GR-3
Similar to the GR-2 except: single selective trigger
**Estimated Value:** $500.00 - $625.00

### Beretta GR-4
Similar to the GR-3 except: automatic ejectors; engraving and deluxe wood
**Estimated Value:** $610.00 - $760.00

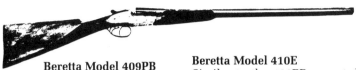

**Beretta Model 409PB**

**Beretta Model 410E**
Similar to the 409PB except: higher quality finish and engraving; automatic ejectors
**Estimated Value: $660.00 - $820.00**

**Beretta Model 409PB**
**Gauge:** 12, 16, 20, or 28
**Action:** Box lock, top lever, break-open; hammerless; double triggers
**Magazine:** None
**Barrel:** Double barrel (side by side); 27½", 28½", or 30"; improved cylinder & modified or modified & full chokes
**Finish:** Blued; checkered walnut straight or pistol grip stock and small tapered forearm; engraved
**Estimated Value: $520.00 - $650.00**

**Beretta Model 411E**
Similar to 410E except: higher quality finish & engraving
**Estimated Value: $880.00 - $1,100.00**

**Beretta Model 410E**

**Beretta Model 410**

**Beretta Model 424**

**Beretta Model 424**
**Gauge:** 12 or 20
**Action:** Box lock; top lever, break-open; hammerless; double trigger
**Magazine:** None
**Barrel:** Double barrel (side by side); chrome lined; matted rib; 26" or 28" improved cylinder & modified or modified & full chokes
**Finish:** Blued; checkered walnut straight grip stock and forearm
**Estimated Value: $630.00 - $790.00**

**Beretta Model 410**
**Gauge:** 10 magnum
**Action:** Box lock; top lever, break-open; hammerless; double triggers
**Magazine:** None
**Barrel:** Double barrel (side by side); 27½", 28½", or 30"; improved cylinder & modified or modified & full chokes
**Finish:** Blued; checkered walnut pistol stock & short tapered forearm
**Estimated Value: $860.00 - $1,075.00**

**Beretta Silver Hawk Featherweight**

**Beretta Model 426**
**Gauge:** 12 or 20; magnum
**Action:** Top lever, break-open; hammerless; single selective trigger; selective automatic ejectors
**Magazine:** None
**Barrel:** Double barrel (side by side); 26" improved cylinder & modified or 28" modified & full; solid rib
**Finish:** Blued; checkered walnut pistol grip stock and tapered forearm; silver gray engraved receiver; silver pigeon inlaid
**Estimated Value: $800.00 - $1,000.00**

**Beretta Silver Hawk Featherweight**
**Gauge:** 12, 16, 20, or 28
**Action:** Box lock; top lever, break-open; hammerless
**Magazine:** None
**Barrel:** Double barrel (side by side); 26"or 32"; variety of chokes; matted rib
**Finish:** Blued; checkered walnut pistol grip stock and forearm
**Estimated Value: $460.00 - $575.00**

**Beretta Silver Hawk Featherweight Magnum**
Similar to the Silver Hawk Featherweight except: 10 or 12 gauge magnum; chrome lined 30" or 32" barrels; ventilated rib; recoil pad
**Estimated Value: $520.00 - $650.00**

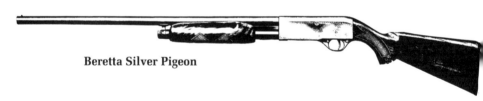

**Beretta Silver Pigeon**

**Beretta Silver Pigeon**
**Gauge:** 12
**Action:** Slide action; hammerless
**Magazine:** 5-shot tubular
**Barrel:** 26"or 32"; various chokes
**Finish:** Blued; engraved and inlaid with silver pigeon; chrome trigger; checkered walnut pistol grip stock and slide handle
**Estimated Value: $260.00 - $325.00**

**Beretta Gold Pigeon**
Similar to the Silver Pigeon except: heavier engraving; gold pigeon inlaid; ventilated rib; gold trigger
**Estimated Value: $550.00 - $690.00**

**Beretta Ruby Pigeon**
Similar to the Gold Pigeon except: deluxe engraving; inlaided pigeon has ruby eye
**Estimated Value: $635.00 - $795.00**

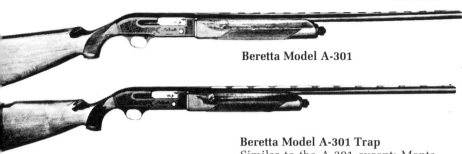

Beretta Model A-301

Beretta Model A-301 Trap

**Beretta Model A-301 Trap**
Similar to the A-301 except: Monte
Carlo stock, recoil pad & gold plated
trigger; 12 gauge only; 30" full choke
**Estimated Value: $345.00 - $430.00**

**Beretta Model A-301**
**Gauge:** 12 or 20; regular or magnum;
add $45.00 for magnum
**Action:** Gas operated, semi-
automatic; hammerless
**Magazine:** 3-shot tubular
**Barrel:** 26" improved cylinder; 28"
modified or full; 30" full in 12 gauge;
ventilated rib; chrome molydenum
**Finish:** Blued; checkered walnut
pistol grip stock and forearm;
decorated alloy receiver; recoil pad
on magnum model
**Estimated Value: $320.00 - $400.00**

**Beretta Model A-301 Skeet**
Similar to the A-301 Trap except:
26" skeet choke barrel
**Estimated Value: $340.00 - $425.00**

**Beretta Model A-301 Deer Gun**
Similar to the A-301 except: 22"
slug barrel; adjustable open sights
**Estimated Value: $325.00 - $410.00**

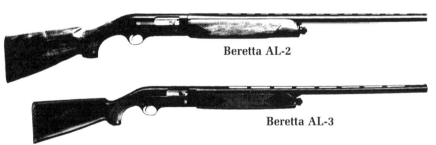

Beretta AL-2

Beretta AL-3

**Beretta AL-3**
Similar to the AL-2 except: light
engraving
**Estimated Value: $300.00 - $380.00**

**Beretta AL-1**
**Gauge:** 12 or 20; regular or magnum
**Action:** Gas operated, semi-
automatic; hammerless
**Magazine:** 3-shot tubular
**Barrel:** 26" or 30"; improved
cylinder, modified full or skeet,
chokes; ventilated rib
**Finish:** Blued; checkered walnut
pistol grip stock and forearm
**Estimated Value: $260.00 - $325.00**

**Beretta AL-2**
Similar to the AL-1 except:
ventilated rib; recoil pad; chrome
lined bore
**Estimated Value: $290.00 - $360.00**

# Beretta

**Beretta Silver Lark**
**Gauge:** 12
**Action:** Gas operated, semi-automatic; hammerless
**Magazine:** 5-shot tubular
**Barrel:** 26"-32", improved cylinder, modified or full chokes
**Finish:** Blued; checkered walnut pistol grip stock and forearm
**Estimated Value:** $265.00 - $330.00

**Beretta Gold Lark**
Similar to the Silver Lark with high-quality engraving and ventilated rib
**Estimated Value:** $360.00 - $450.00

**Beretta Ruby Lark**
Similar to the Silver Lark with deluxe engraving and a stainless steel barrel
**Estimated Value:** $480.00 - $600.00

Beretta Model A302 Mag-Action

**Beretta Model A302 Skeet**
Similar to the Model A302 Mag-Action except: 26" skeet choke barrel
**Estimated Value:** $400.00 - $500.00

**Beretta Model A302 Mag-Action**
**Gauge:** 12 or 20; regular or magnum
**Action:** Gas operated, semi-automatic
**Magazine:** 3-shot tubular
**Barrel:** 26" improved cylinder; 28" modified or full; 30" full choke; or changable choke tubes; ventilated rib; add 5% for multi-choke model with four choke tubes
**Finish:** Blued; checkered walnut pistol grip stock and fluted forearm
**Estimated Value:** $380.00 - $475.00

**Beretta Model A302 Trap**
Similar to the Model A302 Mag-Action except: Monte Carlo stock & 30" full choke barrel
**Estimated Value:** $400.00 - $510.00

**Beretta Model A302 Slug**
Similar to the Model A302 Mag-Action except: 22" slug barrel; adjustable front sight, folding leaf rear sight; swivels
**Estimated Value:** $390.00 - $490.00

**Beretta Model 1200F**

**Beretta Model 1200,
1200 Riot, & 1201**
**Gauge:** 12 regular or magnum
**Action:** Gas operated, semi-automatic
**Magazine:** 3-shot tubular; 7-shot in riot model
**Barrel:** 24", 26", or 28" modified, full, or changeable choke tubes; 20" cylinder bore on Riot Model; add 5% for Riot Model
**Finish:** Blued, non-glare; synthetic stock & forearm
**Estimated Value: $375.00 - $470.00**

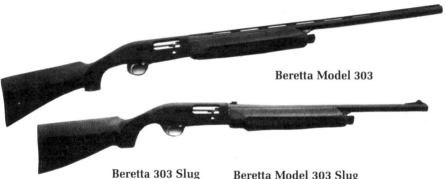

**Beretta Model 303**

**Beretta 303 Slug**

**Beretta Model 303 Slug**
Similar to the Model 303 except: 22" cylinder bore barrel, with rifle sights
**Estimated Value: $415.00 - $520.00**

**Beretta Model 303**
**Gauge:** 12 or 20; regular or magnum
**Action:** Gas operated, semi-automatic
**Magazine:** 2-shot plugged tubular
**Barrel:** 26", 28", 30", or 32" in a variety of chokes or interchangeable choke tubes; deduct 6% for guns without interchangeable choke tubes; 24" barrel on youth model
**Finish:** Blued; checkered walnut pistol grip stock & forearm; recoil pad on youth model; add 14% for Sporting Clays Model
**Estimated Value: $440.00 - $550.00**

**Beretta Model 303 Skeet**
Similar to the Model 303 except: 26" skeet choke barrel
**Estimated Value: $440.00 - $550.00**

**Beretta Model 303 Trap**
Similar to the Model 303 except: 30" or 32" full choke barrel or interchangeable choke tubes; add 6% for set interchangeable choke tubes
**Estimated Value: $440.00 - $550.00**

**Beretta Model A 390 ST**
**Gauge:** 12, regular or magnum
**Action:** Gas operated, semi-automatic; a self-compensating gas operating system performs with any 12 gauge factory load
**Magazine:** 3-shot tubular
**Barrel:** 24", 26", 28", or 30" with mobilchoke screw-in choke tubes; ventilated rib
**Finish:** Black; checkered walnut pistol grip stock & forearm; a new stock drop system and cast-off spacer allows for stock adjustment
**Estimated Value: $470.00 - $585.00**

**Beretta Model A 390 ST Slug**
Same as Model A 390 ST except: 20" or 22" barrel; fixed choke; plain barrel with hook-in bases for scope mounting; blade front sight and adjustable rear
**Estimated Value: $440.00 - $550.00**

**Beretta Model A 304 Ultralight**
Similar to the Model A 390 except: 12 gauge 2¾ only; doesn't use the self compensating gas system
**Estimated Value: $440.00 - $550.00**

**Beretta Model A 390 ST**

# Bernardelli

**Bernardelli Roma**
**Gauge:** 12, 16, 20, or 28
**Action:** Anson & Deeley type; top lever break-open; hammerless; double trigger; automatic ejector
**Magazine:** None
**Barrel:** Double barrel; 27½" or 29½" modified & full choke
**Finish:** Blued; checkered walnut straight or pistol grip stock & forearm; produced in three grades; add $50.00 for single trigger
**Estimated Value:**
　　Roma 3: $650.00 -　$800.00
　　Roma 4: $750.00 - $1,000.00
　　Roma 5: $825.00 - $1,025.00

**Bernardelli Roma**

**Bernardelli Game Cock**
**Gauge:** 12 or 20
**Action:** Box lock; top lever break-open; double trigger; hammerless
**Magazine:** None
**Barrel:** Double barrel; 25" improved & modified or 28" modified & full chokes
**Finish:** Blued; checkered walnut straight stock & forearm; light engraving
**Estimated Value: $600.00 - $750.00**

**Bernardelli Game Cock Deluxe**
Same as the Game Cock with light scroll engraving; single trigger; automatic ejectors
**Estimated Value: $640.00 - $800.00**

**Bernardelli Game Cock Premier**
Same as the Game Cock with more engraving; selective single trigger; automatic ejectors
**Estimated Value: $760.00 - $950.00**

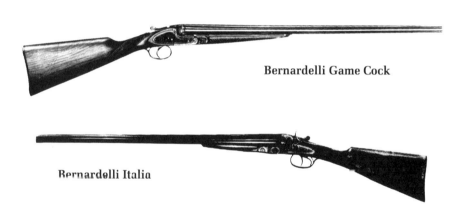

Bernardelli Game Cock

Bernardelli Italia

Bernardelli Brescia

**Bernardelli Italia**
**Gauge:** 12, 16, or 20
**Action:** Top lever break-open; exposed hammer; double trigger
**Magazine:** None
**Barrel:** Double barrel; chrome lined 30" modified & full chokes
**Finish:** Blued; engraved receiver; checkered walnut straight grip stock & forearm
**Estimated Value: $850.00 - $1,065.00**

**Bernardelli Brescia**
Same as the Italia except: 28" barrels; 26" barrels in 20 gauge; modified & improved cylinder bore
**Estimated Value: $600.00 - $800.00**

# Bernardelli/Breda

Bernardelli Holland

Bernardelli Holland

## Bernardelli Holland
**Gauge:** 12
**Action:** top lever break-open; hammerless; double trigger; automatic ejectors
**Magazine:** None
**Barrel:** Double barrel, 26" to 32" any choke combination
**Finish:** Blued; straight or pistol grip stock & forearm; engraving
**Estimated Value: $1,500.00 - $2,000.00**

Bernardelli Holland Deluxe

## Bernardelli Holland Deluxe
Same as the Holland with engraved hunting scene
**Estimated Value: $1,900.00 - $2,500.00**

## Bernardelli St. Uberto
**Gauge:** 12, 16, 20, or 28
**Action:** Box lock; top lever break-open; double triggers; hammerless
**Magazine:** None
**Barrel:** Double barrel, 26" to 32", any choke combination
**Finish:** Blued; checkered walnut straight or pistol grip stock & forearm
**Estimated Value: $725.00 - $910.00**

Bernardelli St. Uberto

# Breda

Breda Autoloading

## Breda Autoloading
**Gauge:** 12 regular or magnum; add 30% for magnum
**Action:** Semi-automatic; hammerless
**Magazine:** 4-shot tubular
**Barrel:** 25½" or 27½"
**Finish:** Blued; checkered walnut straight or pistol grip stock & forearm; available with ribbed barrel; engraving on grades 1, 2, & 3; engraved models worth more; estimated value for plain models
**Estimated Value: $275.00 - $350.00**

Browning BT-99 Trap

## Browning BT-99 Trap
**Gauge:** 12
**Action:** Top lever break-open; automatic ejector; hammerless; single shot
**Magazine:** None
**Barrel:** 32" or 34" full, modified, or improved modified choke; or choke tubes; add 2% for choke tubes; high post ventilated rib
**Finish:** Blued; wide rib; checkered walnut pistol grip stock & forearm, some with Monte Carlo stock; recoil pad; some engraving; Pigeon Grade is satin gray steel with deep relief hand engraving
**Estimated Value: $720.00 - $900.00**

## Browning Model BT-99 Plus
**Gauge:** 12
**Action:** Top lever, break-open; automatic ejector; hammerless; single shot
**Magazine:** None
**Barrel:** 32" or 34", choke tubes; high post, ventilated, tapered target rib with matted sight plane; front & center sight beads; ported barrel optional; add 1% for ported barrel
**Finish:** Blued; receiver engraved with rosette & scrolls; select walnut, checkered pistol grip stock & modified beavertail forearm; Monte Carlo style comb with recoil reducer system; adjustable for drop, cant, cast & length of pull; recoil pad
**Estimated Value: $1,065.00 - $1,335.00**

Browning Superposed

## Browning Superposed Magnum Grade I
Same as the Superposed except: chambered for 3" magnum 12 gauge & recoil pad
**Estimated Value: $1,200.00 - $3,600.00**

## Browning Superposed
**Gauge:** 12, 20, 28, or 410
**Action:** Non-selective trigger; double triggers; or selective trigger
**Magazine:** None
**Barrel:** Browning over & under double barrel; 26½", 28", 30", or 32"; any choke combination; ventilated or matted rib
**Finish:** Blued; hand-checkered European walnut pistol grip stock & forearm; fluted comb; recoil pad; engraving; made in many different grades; more inlays & engraving on higher grades
**Estimated Value: $750.00 - $5,000.00**

# Browning

## Browning Super Light
Similar to Superposed except: lightweight; 26½" barrel; straight grip stock; many grades
**Estimated Value: $1,500.00 - $5,000.00**

## Browning Superposed Broadway Trap Grade I
Similar to Superposed except: wide ventilated rib; many grades
**Estimated Value: $1,400.00 - $4,000.00**

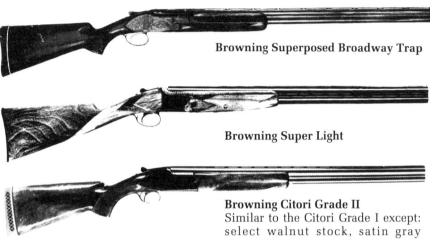

**Browning Superposed Broadway Trap**

**Browning Super Light**

**Browning Citori Grade I**

## Browning Citori Grade II
Similar to the Citori Grade I except: select walnut stock, satin gray receiver engraved with Canada Goose & Ringneck Pheasant scenes; add 5% for 410 or 28 ga.
**Estimated Value: $730.00 - $975.00**

## Browning Citori Grade I
**Gauge:** 12, 20, 28, or 410; regular & magnum; add 3% for 410 or 28 ga.
**Action:** Top lever break-open; hammerless; single selective trigger; automatic ejectors
**Magazine:** None
**Barrel:** Over & under double barrel; 26", 28, or 30" in a variety of choke combinations; or changable choke tubes; ventilated rib
**Finish:** Blued; checkered walnut stock & forearm; Hunting Model has pistol grip stock & beavertail forearm; Sporter has straight stock & lipped forearm; engraved receiver; high-polish finish on Hunting Model, oil finish on Sporter; Upland Special has straight stock; Lighting Model has rounded pistol grip; add 4% for Superlight or Upland Special
**Estimated Value: $665.00 - $830.00**

## Browning Citori Grade III
Similar to the Grade II with grayed receiver, scroll engraving & mallards & ringnecks decoration; 20, 28, & 410 ga. have quail & grouse; add 10% for 28 or 410 ga.
**Estimated Value: $985.00 - $1230.00**

## Browning Citori Grade V
Similar to the Citori Grade II with hand-checkered wood, hand-engraved receiver with Mallard Duck & Ringneck Pheasant scenes; add 5% for 410 or 28 gauge; add 3% for "Invector" choke tubes
**Estimated Value: $1,100.00 - $1,475.00**

Browning Citori Trap

**Browning Citori Sideplate**
Similar to the Citori Grade V in 20 gauge Sporter style only; 26" improved cylinder & modified or modified & full choke; sideplates & receiver are decorated with etched upland game scenes of doves, Ruffed Grouse, quail, & pointing dog
Estimated Value: $1,100.00 - $1,475.00

**Browning Citori Skeet**
Similar to the Citori Grade I except: 26" or 28" skeet choke barrels; high post target rib; add 43% for Grade II or Grade III decoration; add 100% for Grade VI
Estimated Value: $750.00 - $ 940.00

**Browning Citori Trap**
A trap version of the Citori Grade I in 12 gauge only; high post target rib; 30", 32", or 34" barrel; Monte Carlo stock; add 43% for Grade II or Grade III decoration; 100% for Grade VI
Estimated Value: $750.00 - $ 940.00

**Browning Citori Grade VI**
Similar to the Grade V Citori with grayed or blued receiver, deep relief engraving, gold plating & engraving of ringneck pheasants, mallard drakes & English Setter; add 10% for 28 gauge or 410
Estimated Value: $1415.00 - $1,770.00

**Browning Citori Plus**
Gauge: 12
Action: Top lever, break-open; hammerless; automatic ejectors
Magazine: None
Barrel: 30" or 32" over & under double barrel with high post, ventilated, tapered target rib; matted sight plane; choke tubes; front & center sight beads; ported barrel optional; add $50.00 for ported barrel
Finish: Blued; receiver engraving; select walnut checkered pistol grip stock & modified beavertail forearm; Monte Carlo style comb with recoil reduction system adjustable for drop, cant, cast & length of pull; recoil pad
Estimated Value: $1,135.00 - $1,415.00

# Browning

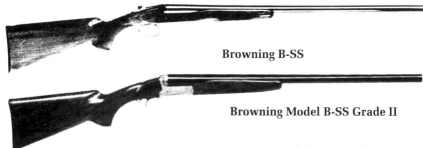

Browning B-SS

Browning Model B-SS Grade II

### Browning B-SS
**Gauge:** 12 or 20
**Action:** Top lever break-open; hammerless; automatic ejectors; barrel selector; add 5% for barrel selector
**Magazine:** None
**Barrel:** Double barrel (side by side); 26", 28", or 30" in many choke combinations
**Finish:** Blued; checkered walnut pistol grip stock & forearm
**Estimated Value: $435.00 - $580.00**

### Browning Model B-SS Grade II
Similar to the B-SS with engraved satin gray frame featuring a pheasant, ducks, and quail
**Estimated Value: $650.00 - $850.00**

### Browning B-SS Sidelock
Similar to the Model B-SS with sidelock action, engraved gray receiver, double triggers, small tapered forearm & straight grip stock
**Estimated Value: $915.00 - $1,280.00**

Browning BPS

### Browning BPS
**Gauge:** 10, 12, or 20; regular or magnum; add 32% for 10 gauge
**Action:** Slide action; concealed hammer; bottom ejection
**Magazine:** 4-shot; 3-shot in magnum
**Barrel:** 26", 28", 30" or 32" in many cokes; or choke tubes; ventilated rib
**Finish:** Blued; checkered walnut pistol grip stock & slide handle; trap Model has Monte Carlo stock; add 5% for Trap Model; Stalker Model has graphite-fiberglass composite stock with matte finish
**Estimated Value: $265.00 - $330.00**

### Browning BPS Buck Special
Similar to the BPS with a 24" barrel for slugs; rifle sights; add 5% for strap & swivels
**Estimated Value: $270.00 - $335.00**

### Browning BPS Youth and Ladies
Similar to the Model BPS in 20 gauge only with 22" barrel, compact stock & recoil pad
**Estimated Value: $265.00 - $330.00**

**Browning BPS Upland Special**

**Browning BPS Upland Special**
Similar to the BPS with a straight grip stock, 22" barrel and "Invector" choke tubes
Estimated Value: $265.00 - $330.00

**Browning BPS Pigeon Grade Hunting**
Same as the BPS except: 12 gauge only; select, high-grade stock and gold trim receiver; Invector chokes.
Estimated Value: $360.00 - $450.00

**Browning BPS Deer Special**
Similar to the BPS except: 12 gauge only; 20" barrel with 5" rifled slug choke tube; adjustable rear sight; scope mount base
Estimated Value: $300.00 - $375.00

**Browning BPS Turkey Special**
Similar to the BPS except: 12 gauge only; 20" barrel with newly designed extra full choke tube; receiver drilled and tapped for scope base
Estimated Value: $280.00 - $350.00

**Browning Model 12**

**Browning Model 42, Grades I & V**
Same as Browning Model 12, Grades I & V except: 410 gauge with 3" chamber; add 70% for Grade V
Estimated Value: $480.00 - $600.00

**Browning Model 12, Grades I & V**
**Gauge:** 20 or 28
**Action:** Slide action, repeating; concealed hammer
**Magazine:** 5-shot tubular; 2-shot with plug
**Barrel:** 26" modified, high ventilated rib
**Finish:** Blued; checkered walnut pistol grip stock & slide handle; Grade V has engraved receiver with gold plated scenes; add 60% for Grade V
Estimated Value: $440.00 - $550.00

# Browning

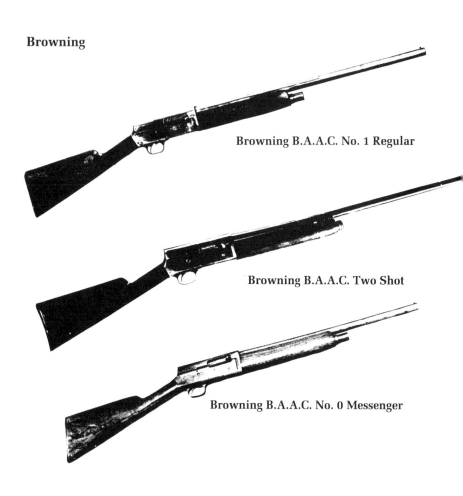

Browning B.A.A.C. No. 1 Regular

Browning B.A.A.C. Two Shot

Browning B.A.A.C. No. 0 Messenger

**Browning B.A.A.C. No. 1 Regular**
**Gauge:** 12
**Action:** Semi-automatic, hammerless
**Magazine:** 4-shot
**Barrel:** 28"
**Finish:** Blued; walnut straight stock
& grooved forearm
**Estimated Value: $280.00 - $350.00**

**Browning B.A.A.C. No. 2 Trap**
Trap Grade version of the No. 1 with
some checkering
**Estimated Value: $310.00 - $390.00**

**Browning B.A.A.C. Two Shot**
Similar to the No. 1 except: 2-shot
model
**Estimated Value: $240.00 - $300.00**

**Browning B.A.A.C. No. 0 Messenger**
A short, 20" barrel, version of the
No. 1, made for bank guards, etc.
**Estimated Value: $260.00 - $325.00**

**F.N. Browning Automatic**
Similar to the B.A.A.C. No. 1 sold
only overseas; some models have
sling swivels
**Estimated Value: $300.00 - $375.00**

**Browning Automatic 5 Standard Grade**

**Browning Automatic 5 Standard Grade**
**Gauge:** 12, 16 , 20, or 410
**Action:** Semi-auto; hammerless; side ejection; recoiling barrel
**Magazine:** 4-shot, bottom load; 3-shot model also available
**Barrel:** 26"-32" full choke, modified or cylinder bore; plain, raised matted rib or ventilated rib; add 13% for ventilated rib
**Finish:** Blued; checkered walnut, pistol grip stock & forearm
**Estimated Value: $490.00 - $600.00**

**Browning Automatic 5 Grades II, III, IV**
Basically the same as the Standard Grade with engraving & improved quality on higher grades; add $50.00 for ventilated rib
**Estimated Value: $500.00 - $2,000.00**

**Browning Automatic-5 Light 12**

**Browning Automatic-5 Light 20**

**Browning Auto-5 Trap**
Basically the same as the Standard Grade except 12 gauge only; trap stock; 30" full choke barrel; ventilated rib; add 35% for Belgian-made.
**Estimated Value: $440.00 - $550.00**

**Browning Auto-5 Light 12**
Basically the same as the Standard Grade except: 12 gauge only & lightweight; add 25% for Belgian-made; stalker model has graphite composite stock and non-glare finish
**Estimated Value: $430.00 - $540.00**

**Browning Auto-5 Light Skeet**
Similar to the Light 12 & Light 20 with 26" or 28" skeet choke barrel; add 35% for Belgian-made
**Estimated Value: $360.00 - $450.00**

**Browning Auto-5 Light 20**
Basically the same as the Standard Grade except: 20 gauge only; lightweight 26" or 28" barrel; add 25% for Belgian-made
**Estimated Value: $430.00 - $540.00**

# Browning

**Browning Automatic-5 Light Buck Special**

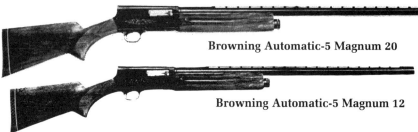

**Browning Automatic-5 Magnum 20**

**Browning Automatic-5 Magnum 12**

**Browning Auto-5 Magnum 20**
Similar to the Standard Model except 20 gauge magnum; 26" or 28" barrel; add 25% for Belgian-made
**Estimated Value: $445.00 - $560.00**

**Browning Auto-5 Magnum 12**
Similar to the Standard Model except: 12 gauge magnum with recoil pad; 32" full choke barrel; add 25% for Belgian-made; stalker model has graphite composite stock and non-glare finish
**Estimated Value: $445.00 - $560.00**

**Browning Auto-5 Light Buck Special**
Similar to the Standard Model 12 or 20 gauge except: special 24" barrel choked & bored for slug; add 4% for strap & swivels; add 25% for Belgian-made
**Estimated Value: $435.00 - $545.00**

**Browning Auto-5 Buck Special Magnum**
Same as the Buck Special except: 3" magnum in 12 & 20 gauge; add 4% for strap & swivels; add 25% for Belgian-made
**Estimated Value: $450.00 - $560.00**

**Browning Automatic 5 Sweet Sixteen**

**Browning Auto-5 Sweet Sixteen**
A lightweight 16 gauge version of the Standard Model Auto-5 with a gold plated trigger. Made from about 1936 to 1975 in Belgium; add 25% for Belgium-made
**Estimated Value: $430.00 - $540.00**

**Browning Special (American-Made)**
Similar to Grade I with a matted or ventilated rib
**Estimated Value: $310.00 - $390.00**

**Browning Grade I (American Made)**

**Browning Grade I (American-Made)**
Similar to Browning Standard Grade except: made by Remington from 1940 until about 1948. World War II forced the closing of the plant in Belgium
**Estimated Value: $280.00 - $350.00**

**Browning Special Skeet (American-Made)**
Same as the Grade I with a Cutts Compensator
**Estimated Value: $300.00 - $375.00**

**Browning Utility (American-Made)**
Similar to Grade I with Poly-Choke
**Estimated Value: $240.00 - $300.00**

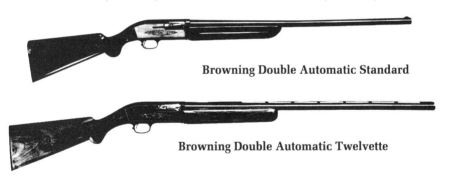

**Browning Double Automatic Standard**

**Browning Double Automatic Twelvette**

**Browning Double Automatic Twelvette**
Basically the same as the Standard with lightweight aluminum receiver
**Estimated Value: $360.00 - $450.00**

**Browning Double Automatic Twentyweight**
A still lighter version of the Standard in 20 ga. with 26½" barrel
**Estimated Value: $365.00 - $460.00**

**Browning Double Automatic Standard**
**Gauge:** 12
**Action:** Semi-automatic; short recoil, side ejection; hammerless; 2-shot
**Magazine:** 1-shot
**Barrel:** 30" or 28" full choke; 28" or 26" modified choke; 28" or 26" skeet choke; 26" cylinder bore or improved cylinder; ventilated rib optional
**Finish:** Blued; checkered walnut pistol grip stock & forearm; add 8% for ventilated rib
**Estimated Value: $320.00 - $400.00**

# Browning

Browning 2000

Browning Model B-2000 Trap

**Browning Model B-2000
Trap & Skeet**
Similar to the B-2000 with options of high-post ventilated rib & recoil pad on Trap Model.
**Estimated Value: $300.00 - $400.00**

**Browning 2000 or B-2000**
Similar to the Automatic 5 except: gas operated; in 12 or 20 gauge regular or magnum
**Estimated Value: $280.00 - $375.00**

**Browning 2000 Buck Special**
Similar to the 2000 except; 24" barrel; adjustable rifle sights; swivels
**Estimated Value: $350.00 - $425.00**

Browning B-80

**Browning B-80 Buck Special**
Similar to the B-80 except: 24" slug barrel; rifle sights; add $20.00 for strap & swivels
**Estimated Value: $325.00 - $425.00**

**Browning B-80 Upland Special**
Similar to the Model B-80 except: straight grip stock; 22" barrel
**Estimated Value: $335.00 - $420.00**

**Browning B-80, B-80 Plus**
**Gauge:** 12 or 20; regular or magnum
**Action:** Semi-automatic; gas operated
**Magazine:** 3-shot, 2-shot in magnum
**Barrel:** 26", 28", 30", or 32" in a variety of chokes or choke tubes; internally chrome plated; ventilated rib
**Finish:** Blued; checkered walnut semi-pistol grip stock & fluted, checkered forearm; alloy receiver on Superlight Model (B-80 Plus)
**Estimated Value: $335.00 - $420.00**

**Browning Model A-500**

**Browning Model A-500**
**Gauge:** 12; regular or magnum
**Action:** Short recoil operated semi-automatic
**Magazine:** 4-shot tubular; 3-shot in magnum; magazine cut-off allows chambering of shell independent of magazine
**Barrel:** 26", 28", or 30" with choke tubes; ventilated rib; 24" Buck Special barrel optional
**Finish:** Blued; checkered walnut pistol grip stock & forearm; recoil pad
**Estimated Value: $330.00 - $415.00**

**Browning Model A-500G**

**Browning Model A-500R**
**Gauge:** 12; regular or magnum
**Action:** Recoil operated, semi-automatic
**Magazine:** 4-shot; 3-shot in magnum
**Barrel:** 26", 28", or 30" with choke tubes; ventilated rib with matted sighting surface
**Finish:** Blued; red accents on receiver; select checkered walnut pistol grip stock & forearm; gold plated trigger
**Estimated Value: $335.00 - $420.00**

**Browning Model A-500R Buck Special**
Similar to the Model A-500R except: 24" slug barrel; adjustable rear sight
**Estimated Value: $355.00 - $445.00**

**Browning Model A-500G**
**Gauge:** 12; regular or magnum
**Action:** Gas operated, semi-automatic
**Magazine:** 4-shot; 3-shot in magnum shells
**Barrel:** 26", 28", or 30" barrel with choke tubes; ventilated rib with matted sighting surface
**Finish:** Blued; gold accents on receiver; select checkered walnut, pistol grip & forearm; recoil pad; gold trigger
**Estimated Value: $385.00 - $480.00**

**Browning Model A-500G Buck Special**
Similar to the Model A-500G except: 24" slug barrel & adjustable rear sight
**Estimated Value: $400.00 - $500.00**

# Charles Daly

Charles Daly Single Barrel Trap

**Charles Daly Commander 100**
**Gauge:** 12, 16, 20, 28, or 410
**Action:** Box lock; top lever, break-open; hammerless; automatic ejectors
**Magazine:** None
**Barrel:** Over & under double barrel; 26", 28", or 30" improved cylinder & modified or modified & full chokes
**Finish:** Blued; checkered walnut straight or pistol grip stock & forearm; engraved
**Estimated Value: $450.00 - $600.00**

**Charles Daly Commander 200**
A fancier version of the Commander 100 with select wood, more engraving & a higher quality finish
**Estimated Value: $620.00 - $775.00**

**Charles Daly Single Barrel Trap**
**Gauge:** 12
**Action:** Box lock; top lever, break-open; hammerless; single shot
**Magazine:** None; single shot
**Barrel:** 32" or 34" full choke; ventilated rib
**Finish:** Blued; checkered walnut Monte Carlo pistol grip stock & beavertail forearm; recoil pad. This model should not be confused with the Single Barrel Trap Models made in the 1930's that are worth several times more
**Estimated Value: $380.00 - $475.00**

**Charles Daly Hammerless Double**
**Gauge:** 10, 12, 16, 20, 28 or 410
**Action:** Box lock; top lever, break-open; hammerless; automatic ejectors (except Superior)
**Magazine:** None
**Barrel:** Double barrel (side by side); 26", 28", 30", or 32"; many choke combinations
**Finish:** Blued; checkered walnut pistol grip stock & short tapered forearm; engraving; manufactured in many different grades; alike except for quality of finish & amount of engraving
**Estimated Value: $1,200.00 - $4,500.00**

Charles Daly

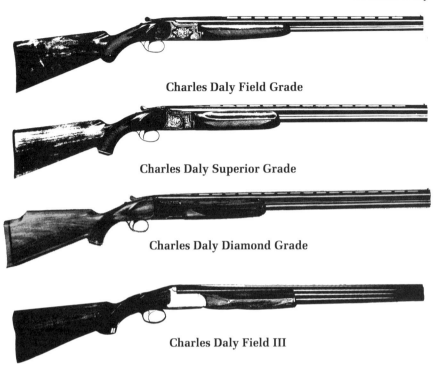

Charles Daly Field Grade

Charles Daly Superior Grade

Charles Daly Diamond Grade

Charles Daly Field III

**Charles Daly Field Grade**
**Gauge:** 12, 20, 28, or 410 regular; 12
or 20 magnum
**Action:** Box lock; top lever, break-
open; hammerless; single trigger
**Magazine:** None
**Barrel:** Over & under double barrel;
26", 28", or 30"; many choke combinations; ventilated rib
**Finish:** Blued; engraved; checkered
walnut pistol grip stock & forearm;
12 gauge magnum has recoil pad
**Estimated Value:** $410.00 - $550.00

**Charles Daly Superior Grade**
Similar to the Field Grade except:
not chambered for magnum
**Estimated Value:** $430.00 - $575.00

**Charles Daly Diamond Grade**
Similar to the Superior with select
wood & fancier engraving
**Estimated Value:** $560.00 - $700.00

**Charles Daly Field III**
Similar to the Field Grade with some
minor changes; double trigger
**Estimated Value:** $265.00 - $335.00

**Charles Daly Superior II**
Similar to the Field III but higher
quality
**Estimated Value:** $420.00 - $525.00

# Charles Daly

Charles Daly Venture Grade

Charles Daly Auto

Charles Daly Auto Superior

**Charles Daly Venture Grade**
**Gauge:** 12 or 20
**Action:** Box lock; top lever, break-open; hammerless; automatic ejectors
**Magazine:** None
**Barrel:** Over & under double barrel; 26", 28", or 30", various chokes; ventilated rib
**Finish:** Blued; checkered walnut pistol grip stock & forearm; add $25.00 for Skeet Model; add $35.00 for Trap Model
**Estimated Value: $340.00 - $425.00**

**Charles Daly Auto Field**
**Gauge:** 12 regular or magnum
**Action:** Semi-automatic, recoil operated
**Magazine:** 5-shot tubular
**Barrel:** 26" improved cylinder or skeet, 28" modified or full, 30" full, choke; ventilated rib
**Finish:** Blued; checkered walnut pistol grip stock & forearm
**Estimated Value: $240.00 - $300.00**

**Charles Daly Auto Superior**
Similar to the Auto Field but higher quality
**Estimated Value: $260.00 - $325.00**

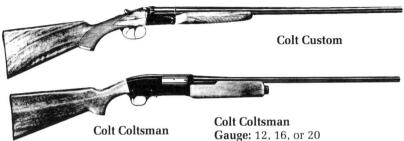

Colt Custom

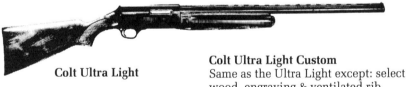

Colt Coltsman

## Colt Custom
**Gauge:** 12 or 16
**Action:** Box lock; top lever, break-open; hammerless; double trigger; automatic ejectors
**Magazine:** None
**Barrel:** Double barrel (side by side); 26" improved & modified, 28" modified & full or 30" full chokes
**Finish:** Blued; checkered walnut pistol grip stock & tapered forearm
**Estimated Value: $300.00 - $390.00**

## Colt Coltsman
**Gauge:** 12, 16, or 20
**Action:** Side action
**Magazine:** 4-shot
**Barrel:** 26" improved, 28" modified, 30" full choke
**Finish:** Blued; plain walnut pistol grip stock & slide handle
**Estimated Value: $180.00 - $225.00**

## Colt Coltsman Custom
A fancier version of the Coltsman with checkering & ventilated rib
**Estimated Value: $210.00 - $260.00**

Colt Ultra Light

## Colt Ultra Light Custom
Same as the Ultra Light except: select wood, engraving & ventilated rib
**Estimated Value: $250.00 - $320.00**

## Colt Ultra Light
**Gauge:** 12 or 20
**Action:** Semi-automatic
**Magazine:** 4-shot
**Barrel:** Chrome lined; 26" improved or modified; 28" modified or full; 30" or 32" full choke; rib optional; add $15.00 for solid rib; add $25.00 for ventilated rib
**Finish:** Blued; checkered walnut pistol grip stock & forearm; alloy receiver
**Estimated Value: $220.00 - $275.00**

## Colt Magnum Auto
Same as the Ultra Light except: magnum gauges & of heavier weight; add $15.00 for solid rib; add $25.00 for ventilated rib
**Estimated Value: $240.00 - $300.00**

## Colt Magnum Auto Custom
Same as Magnum Auto except: select wood, engraving & ventilated rib
**Estimated Value: $260.00 - $325.00**

# Darne

**Darne Sliding Breech Double**

**Darne Sliding Breech Double**
**Gauge:** 12, 16, 20, or 28
**Action:** Sliding breech; selective ejectors; double trigger
**Magazine:** None
**Barrel:** Double barrel (side by side); 25½" or 27½" modified & improved cylinder choke; raised rib
**Finish:** Blued; checkered walnut straight or pistol grip stock & forearm
**Estimated Value: $600.00 - $800.00**

**Darne Deluxe**
Same as the Sliding Breech Double with engraving & 28" modified & full choke barrels
**Estimated Value: $825.00 - $1,100.00**

**Darne Supreme**
Same as the Darne Deluxe except: 20 or 28 gauge; 25½" barrels; elaborate engraving & swivels
**Estimated Value: $1,200.00 - $1,500.00**

**Darne Deluxe**

Davidson Model 69SL

Davidson Model 63B

Davidson Model 63B Magnum

## Davidson Model 73 Stagecoach
**Gauge:** 12 or 20 magnum
**Action:** Box lock; top lever break open; exposed hammers
**Magazine:** None
**Barrel:** Double barrel (side by side); 20" improved cylinder & modified or modified & full chokes; matted rib
**Finish:** Blued; checkered walnut pistol grip stock & forearm; sights; engraved receiver
**Estimated Value:** $190.00 - $240.00

## Davidson Model 69 SL
**Gauge:** 12 or 20
**Action:** Side lock, hammerless
**Magazine:** None
**Barrel:** Double barrel (side by side); 26", 28", or 30"; variety of chokes
**Finish:** Blued or nickel; checkered walnut pistol grip stock & forearm; gold plated trigger; engraved
**Estimated Value:** $240.00 - $300.00

## Davidson Model 63B
**Gauge:** 12, 16, 20, 28, or 410
**Action:** Box lock; top lever break-open; double triggers
**Magazine:** None
**Barrel:** Double barrel (side by side); 25" (410), 26", 28", or 30" in other gauges; any choke combination
**Finish:** Blued or nickel; checkered walnut pistol grip stock & forearm; some engraving
**Estimated Value:** $220.00 - $275.00

## Davidson Model 63B Magnum
Same as Model 63B except: 10, 12, or 20 gauge magnum; available with 32" barrel in 10 gauge
**Estimated Value:** $235.00 - $295.00

# Fox

## Fox Trap (Single Barrel)

**Gauge:** 12
**Action:** Box lock; top lever break-open; hammerless; automatic ejector; single shot
**Magazine:** None; single shot
**Barrel:** 30" or 32" trap bore; ventilated rib
**Finish:** Blued; checkered walnut half or full pistol grip stock & forearm; decorated receiver; grades differ in quality of craftsmanship & decoration; some have Monte Carlo stock; ME Grade was made to order with inlaid gold & finest walnut wood
**Estimated Value:**
  **GRADES**
    **JE: $1,200.00 - $1,600.00**
    **KE: $1,400.00 - $2,000.00**
    **LE: $1,400.00 - $2,500.00**
    **ME: $4,000.00 - $5,500.00**

**Fox Trap (Single Barrel)**

## Fox Sterlingworth

**Gauge:** 12, 16, or 20
**Action:** Box lock; top lever break-open; hammerless; double trigger or selective single trigger; some with automatic ejectors; add 10% for selective trigger; add 12% for automatic ejectors
**Magazine:** None
**Barrel:** Double barrel (side by side); 26", 28", or 30"; full & full, modified & full, cylinder & modified chokes
**Finish:** Blued; checkered walnut pistol grip stock & forearm
**Estimated Value: $490.00 - $600.00**

## Fox Sterlingworth Skeet

Same as the Sterlingworth except: skeet bore; 26" or 28" barrels; straight grip stock; add 12% for automatic ejectors
**Estimated Value: $560.00 - $690.00**

**Fox Sterlingworth**

## Fox Skeeter

Similar to Sterlingworth except: 28" skeet bored barrels; ventilated rib; ivory bead; recoil pad; 12 or 20 gauge; automatic ejectors
**Estimated Value: $750.00 - $1,000.00**

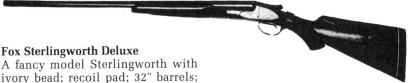

## Fox Sterlingworth Deluxe
A fancy model Sterlingworth with ivory bead; recoil pad; 32" barrels; selective single trigger; add 10% for automatic ejectors
Estimated Value: $575.00 - $700.00

**Fox Sterlingworth Deluxe**

**Fox Model B**

## Fox Model B, BE
**Gauge:** 12, 16, 20, or 410
**Action:** Box lock; top lever break-open; hammerless; double triggers; Model BE has automatic ejectors; add $60.00 for model BE
**Magazine:** None
**Barrel:** Double barrel (side by side); 24", 26", 28", or 30"; in almost any choke combination; ventilated rib
**Finish:** Blued; checkered walnut pistol grip stock & forearm
Estimated Value: $230.00 - $290.00

## Fox Model B Lightweight
Same as the Model B except: 24" cylinder bore & modified choke barrels in 12 & 20 gauge
Estimated Value: $210.00 - $265.00

## Fox Hammerless Doubles
Similar to the Sterlingworth models except: in varying degrees of increased quality. All have automatic ejectors except Grade A; add $60.00 for selective single trigger; $125.00 for ventilated rib
**Estimated Value:**

| Grade | | |
|-------|--------|--------|
| A: | $650.00 - | $850.00 |
| AE: | $950.00 - | $1,200.00 |
| BE: | $1,200.00 - | $1,600.00 |
| CE: | $1,300.00 - | $1,700.00 |
| DE: | $2,275.00 - | $3,000.00 |

## Fox Super Fox
**Gauge:** 12
**Action:** Box lock; top lever break-open; hammerless; double trigger; automatic ejectors
**Magazine:** None
**Barrel:** Double barrel (side by side); 30" or 32" full choke
**Finish:** Blued; checkered walnut pistol grip stock & forearm
Estimated Value: $520.00 - $650.00

# Fox

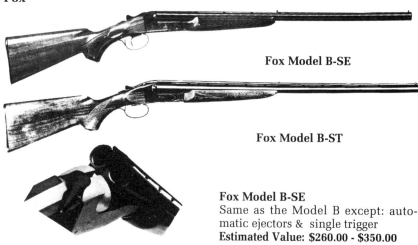

Fox Model B-SE

Fox Model B-ST

Fox Model BDL

**Fox Model B-DL & B-DE**
Similar to the B-ST except: chrome receiver & beavertail forearm
Estimated Value: $275.00 - $350.00

**Fox Model B-SE**
Same as the Model B except: automatic ejectors & single trigger
Estimated Value: $260.00 - $350.00

**Fox Model B-ST**
Same as Model B except: gold plated non-selective single trigger
Estimated Value: $250.00 - $325.00

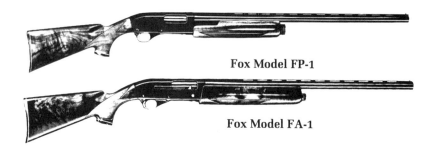

Fox Model FP-1

Fox Model FA-1

**Fox Model FP-1**
Gauge: 12 ( 2¾" or 3")
Action: Slide action, hammerless
Magazine: 4-shot tubular; 3-shot with 3" shells
Barrel: 28" modified; 30" full choke; ventilated rib
Finish: Blued; checkered walnut pistol grip stock & slide handle; rosewood cap with inlay
Estimated Value: $220.00 - $275.00

**Fox Model FA-1**
Gauge: 12 ( 2¾")
Action: Semi-automatic; gas operated
Magazine: 3-shot tubular
Barrel: 28" modified; 30" full choke; ventilated rib
Finish: Blued; checkered walnut pistol grip stock & forearm; rosewood cap with inlay
Estimated Value: $230.00 - $290.00

# Franchi

**Franchi Airone**

**Franchi Airone**
**Gauge:** 12
**Action:** Box lock; top lever, break-open; hammerless; automatic ejectors
**Magazine:** None
**Barrel:** Double barrel (side by side); several lengths & choke combinations
**Finish:** Blued; checkered walnut straight grip stock & short tapered forearm; engraving
**Estimated Value: $700.00 - $875.00**

**Franchi Astore**
**Gauge:** 12
**Action:** Box lock; top lever, break-open; hammerless; double triggers
**Magazine:** None
**Barrel:** Double barrel (side by side); several lengths & choke combinations available
**Finish:** Blued; checkered walnut straight grip stock & short tapered forearm
**Estimated Value: $680.00 - $850.00**

**Franchi Astore S**
Same as the Astore except: higher quality wood & engraving
**Estimated Value: $1,000.00 - $1,250.00**

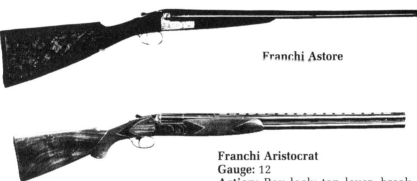

**Franchi Astore**

**Franchi Aristocrat**

**Franchi Aristocrat Skeet**
Same as the Aristocrat Trap except: 26" skeet barrels
**Estimated Value: $540.00 - $675.00**

**Franchi Aristocrat**
**Gauge:** 12
**Action:** Box lock; top lever, break-open; hammerless; automatic ejectors; single trigger
**Magazine:** None
**Barrel:** Over & under double barrel; 24" cylinder bore & improved cylinder; 26" improved cylinder & modified, 28" or 30" modified & full chokes; ventilated rib
**Finish:** Blued; checkered walnut pistol grip stock & forearm; engraving
**Estimated Value: $470.00 - $590.00**

# Franchi

Franchi Aristocrat Trap

**Franchi Aristocrat Silver King**
Similar to the Aristocrat except: higher quality finish; select wood; engraving
**Estimated Value: $580.00 - $725.00**

**Franchi Aristocrat Trap**
Similar to the Aristocrat except: Monte Carlo stock; chrome lined barrels; case hardened receiver; 30" barrels
**Estimated Value: $520.00 - $650.00**

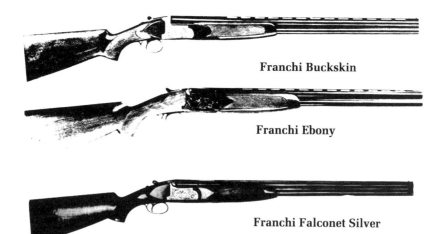

Franchi Buckskin

Franchi Ebony

Franchi Falconet Silver

**Franchi Falconet Buckskin & Ebony**
**Gauge:** 12 or 20
**Action:** Box lock; top lever, break-open; hammerless
**Magazine:** None
**Barrel:** Over & under double barrel; chrome lined; 24", 26", 28", or 30" barrels in several choke combinations; ventilated rib
**Finish:** Blued; colored frame with engraving; epoxy finished checkered walnut pistol grip stock & forearm; Buckskin & Ebony differ only in color of receiver & engraving
**Estimated Value: $470.00 - $590.00**

**Franchi Falconet Silver**
Same as the Falconet Buckskin & Ebony except: 12 gauge only; pickled silver receiver
**Estimated Value: $500.00 - $625.00**

**Franchi Falconet Super**
Similar to the Falconet Silver except: slightly different forearm; 12 gauge only; 27" or 28" barrels
**Estimated Value: $520.00 - $650.00**

**Franchi Peregrine 400**

**Franchi Peregrine 400**
**Gauge:** 12 or 20
**Action:** Box lock; top lever, break-open; hammerless
**Magazine:** None
**Barrel:** Over & under double barrel; 26½", 28" in various chokes; chrome lined; ventilated rib
**Finish:** Blued; checkered walnut pistol grip stock & forearm
**Estimated Value:** $460.00 - $585.00

**Franchi Peregrine 451**
Similar to the 400 except: lightweight alloy receiver
**Estimated Value:** $440.00 - $550.00

**Franchi Peregrine 451**

**Franchi Diamond**
**Gauge:** 12
**Action:** Box lock; top lever, break-open; hammerless; single selective trigger; automatic extractors
**Magazine:** None
**Barrel:** Over & under double barrel; 28" modified & full choke; ventilated rib
**Finish:** Blued; checkered walnut pistol grip stock & forearm; silver plated receiver
**Estimated Value:** $540.00 - $675.00

**Franchi Alcione**
**Gauge:** 12 magnum
**Action:** Box lock; top lever, break-open; hammerless; single selective trigger; automatic split selective ejectors
**Magazine:** None
**Barrel:** Over & under double barrel; 26" improved cylinder & modified; 28" modified & full choke; ventilated rib
**Finish:** Blued; coin-finished steel receiver with scroll engraving; checkered walnut pistol grip stock & forearm; recoil pad
**Estimated Value:** $440.00 - $550.00

# Franchi

**Franchi Standard Model**

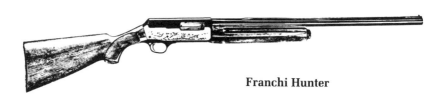

**Franchi Hunter**

**Franchi Standard Model, 48AL**
**Gauge:** 12, 20, or 28
**Action:** Semi-automatic; recoil operated
**Magazine:** 5-shot tubular
**Barrel:** 24" or 26" improved cylinder, modified or skeet; 28" modified or full chokes; chrome lined; ventilated rib on some
**Finish:** Blued; checkered walnut pistol grip stock with fluted forearm
**Estimated Value: $280.00 - $350.00**

**Franchi Hunter, 48AL**
Similar to the Standard Model except: 12 or 20 gauge; higher quality wood; engraving; ventilated rib
**Estimated Value: $300.00 - $390.00**

**Franchi Hunter Magnum**
Same as the Hunter except: recoil pad; chambered for 12 or 20 ga. mag.
**Estimated Value: $320.00 - $400.00**

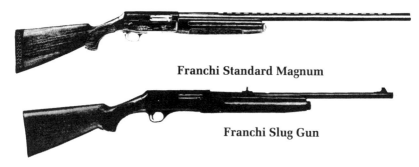

**Franchi Standard Magnum**

**Franchi Slug Gun**

**Franchi Standard Magnum, 48AL**
Similar to the Standard model, 48AL except: recoil pad; chambered for magnum shells; 12 or 20 gauge
**Estimated Value: $300.00 - $375.00**

**Franchi Slug Gun, 48AL**
Similar to the Standard Model, 48AL except: 22" cylinder bore barrel; sights; swivels; alloy receiver 12 or 20 gauge
**Estimated Value: $280.00 - $350.00**

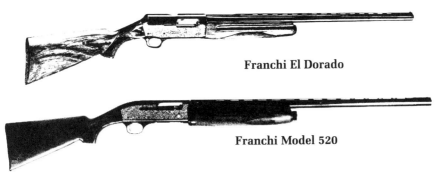

Franchi El Dorado

Franchi Model 520

**Franchi Eldorado**
Similar to the Standard Model, AL
except: heavy engraving; select wood;
gold plated trigger; ventilated rib
**Estimated Value: $380.00 - $475.00**

**Franchi Model 500**
Similar to the Standard model, 48AL
except: gas operated; 12 gauge only;
made for fast takedown
**Estimated Value: $280.00 - $350.00**

**Franchi Model 520**
Similar to the Model 500 with
deluxe features
**Estimated Value: $320.00 - $300.00**

**Franchi Model 530 Trap**
Similar to the Model 520 except:
Monte Carlo stock; high ventilated
rib; three interchangeable choke tubes
**Estimated Value: $440.00 - $550.00**

Franchi Prestige

**Franchi Elite**
Similar to the Prestige with higher
quality finish. Receiver has acid-
etched wildlife scenes
**Estimated Value: $325.00 - $410.00**

**Franchi Prestige, PG 85MA**
**Gauge:** 12  regular or magnum
**Action:** Gas operated, semi-automatic
**Magazine:** 5-shot tubular (2¾"
shells)
**Barrel:** 24" slug; 26" improved
cylinder or modified, 28" modified
or full, 30" full; chrome lined;
ventilated rib
**Finish:** Blued; checkered walnut
pistol grip stock & fluted forearm;
sights on slug barrel
**Estimated Value: $300.00 - $375.00**

# Greifelt

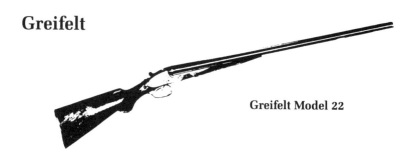

Greifelt Model 22

**Greifelt Model 22**
**Gauge:** 12 or 16
**Action:** Box lock; top lever, break-open; hammerless; double trigger
**Magazine:** None
**Barrel:** Double barrel (side by side); 28" or 30" modified or full chokes
**Finish:** Blued; checkered walnut straight or pistol grip stock & forearm
**Estimated Value:** 1,200.00 - $1,500.00

**Greifelt Model 103**
**Gauge:** 12 or 16
**Action:** Box lock; top lever, break-open; hammerless; double triggers
**Magazine:** None
**Barrel:** Double barrel (side by side); 28" or 30" modified & full chokes
**Finish:** Blued; checkered walnut straight or pistol grip stock & forearm
**Estimated Value:** $1,100.00 - $1,375.00

**Greifelt Model 22E**
Same as Model 22 with automatic ejector
**Estimated Value:** $1,260.00 - $1,575.00

**Greifelt Model 103E**
Same as the Model 103 with automatic ejectors
**Estimated Value:** $1,180.00 - $1,475.00

# Harrington & Richardson

Harrington & Richardson No. 3

**H & R No. 3**
**Gauge:** 12, 16, 20, or 410
**Action:** Box lock; top lever, break-open; hammerless; single shot; automatic extractor
**Magazine:** None
**Barrel:** 26", 28", 30", or 32" full choke
**Finish:** Blued; walnut semi-pistol grip stock & tapered forearm
**Estimated Value:** $75.00 - $95.00

**H & R No. 5**
**Gauge:** 20, 28, or 410
**Action:** Box lock; top lever, break-open; exposed hammer; single shot; automatic extractor
**Magazine:** None
**Barrel:** 26" or 28" full choke
**Finish:** Blued; walnut semi-pistol grip stock & tapered forearm
**Estimated Value: $80.00 - $100.00**

Harrington & Richardson No. 5

**H & R No. 6**
Similar to the No. 5 except: 10, 12, 16, or 20 gauge; heavier design; barrel lengths of 28", 30", 32", 34", or 36"
**Estimated Value: $85.00 - $110.00**

Harrington & Richardson No. 6

**H & R No. 8**
Similar to the No. 6 with different style forearm & in 12, 16, 20, 24, 28 & 410 gauges
**Estimated Value: $65.00 - $80.00**

Harrington & Richardson No. 8

**H & R No. 7 or No. 9**
Similar to the No. 8 with smaller forearm & more rounded pistol grip; not available in 24 gauge
**Estimated Value: $65.00 - $85.00**

Harrington & Richardson No. 7

Harrington & Richardson Topper No. 48

**H & R Topper No. 48**
Similar to the No. 8. Made from the mid 1940's to the late 1950's
**Estimated Value: $70.00 - $90.00**

# Harrington & Richardson

## H & R Topper No. 488 Deluxe
Similar to the No. 48 except: chrome receiver; recoil pad; black lacquered stock & forearm
Estimated Value: $75.00 - $95.00

## H & R Topper Jr. 480
Youth version of the No. 48; 410 gauge; 26" barrel; smaller stock
Estimated Value: $60.00 - $75.00

## H & R Topper Jr. 580
Similar to the Topper Jr. 480 except: color finish similar to 188 Deluxe
Estimated Value: $65.00 - $80.00

## H & R Folding Model
Gauge: 28 or 410 with light frame; 12, 16, 20, 28, or 410 with heavy frame
Action: Box lock; top lever, break-open; exposed hammer; single shot
Magazine: None
Barrel: 22" in light frame; 26" in heavy frame; full choke
Finish: Blued; walnut semi-pistol grip stock & tapered forearm; sight
Estimated Value: $95.00 - $120.00

**Harrington & Richardson Folding Model**

Harrington & Richardson Topper 158

## H & R Topper 188 Deluxe
Similar to the No. 148 with black, red, blue, green, pink, yellow or purple lacquered finish; chrome plated frame; 410 gauge only
Estimated Value: $65.00 - $80.00

## H & R Topper 158 or 058
Gauge: 12, 16, 20, 28, or 410
Action: Box lock; side lever, break-open; exposed hammer; single shot; Also available in 058 combination with 22" rifle barrel in 22 Hornet or 30-30 Win.; add 20% for extra barrel
Magazine: None
Barrel: 28", 30", 32", 34", or 36"; variety of chokes
Finish: Blued; plain wood, straight or semi-pistol grip stock & tapered forearm
Estimated Value: $75.00 - $95.00

## H & R No. 148
Gauge: 12, 16, 20, or 410
Action: Box lock; top lever, break-open; hammerless; single shot; automatic extractor
Magazine: None
Barrel: 28", 30", 32", 34", or 36"; full choke
Finish: Blued; walnut semi-pistol grip stock & forearm; recoil pad
Estimated Value: $70.00 - $85.00

Harrington & Richardson Model 099 Deluxe

Harrington & Richardson Topper 198

Harrington & Richardson Topper 490

Harrington & Richardson Topper Buck 162

### H & R Model 258 Handy Gun
Similar to the Model 058 combination shotgun/rifle with nickel finish; 22" barrel; 20 gauge with 22 Hornet, 30-30, 44 magnum, 357 magnum or 357 Maximum rifle barrel
**Estimated Value: $140.00 - $175.00**

### H & R Topper 490 & 490 Greenwing
A youth version of the Model 158 & 058 with 26" barrel; shorter stock; 20, 28, or 410 gauges only; Greenwing has higher quality finish
**Estimated Value: $65.00 - $85.00**

### H & R Model 099 Deluxe
Similar to the Model 158 with electro-less matte nickel finish
**Estimated Value: $65.00 - $85.00**

### H & R Topper 590
Similar to the 490 with chrome plated receiver & color lacquered stock & forearm
**Estimated Value: $70.00 - $90.00**

### H & R Topper 198 or 098
Similar to the Model 158 or 058 except: 20 or 410 gauge only; black lacquered stock & forearm; nickel plated receiver
**Estimated Value: $ 80.00 - $100.00**

### H & R Topper Buck 162
Similar to the Model 158 & 058 except: 24" cylinder bore barrel for slugs; equipped with sights
**Estimated Value: $ 80.00 - $100.00**

# Harrington & Richardson

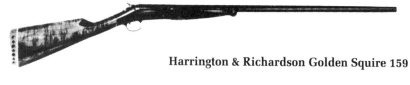

Harrington & Richardson Golden Squire 159

Harrington & Richardson Model 176

## H & R  Golden Squire 159
**Gauge:** 12 or 20
**Action:** Box lock; top lever, break-open; exposed hammer; single shot; automatic ejector
**Magazine:** None
**Barrel:** 28" or 30";  full choke
**Finish:** Blued; wood, straight grip stock & lipped forearm; recoil pad
**Estimated Value:** $80.00 - $100.00

## H & R  Model 176
**Gauge:** 10, 12, 16, or 20  regular or magnum
**Action:** Box lock; top lever, break-open; exposed hammer; single shot
**Magazine:** None
**Barrel:** 32" or 36" full choke in 10 or 12 gauge; 32" full choke in 16 or 20 gauge
**Finish:** Blued; case hardened receiver; plain hardwood Monte Carlo pistol grip stock & forearm; recoil pad
**Estimated Value:** $80.00 - $100.00

## H & R  Golden Squire Jr. 459
Similar to the 159 except: 26" barrel & shorter stock
**Estimated Value:** $75.00 - $95.00

## H & R  Model 176 Slug
Similar to the Model 176 except: 28" cylinder bore slug barrel; rifle sights; swivels
**Estimated Value:** $85.00 - $115.00

Harrington & Richardson Model 088

## H & R  Model 088 Jr.
Similar to the Model 088 with a scaled-down stock & forearm; 25" barrel in 20 or 410 gauge
**Estimated Value:** $75.00 - $95.00

## H & R  Model 088
**Gauge:** 12, 16, 20, or 410 regular or magnum
**Action:** Box lock; top lever, break-open; exposed hammer; single shot
**Magazine:** None
**Barrel:** 28" modified or full in 12 gauge; 28" modified in 16 gauge; 26" modified or full in 20 gauge; 25" full in 410
**Finish:** Blued; case hardened receiver; plain hardwood semi-pistol grip stock & forearm
**Estimated Value:** $70.00 - $90.00

*Pocket Guide to Shotguns*

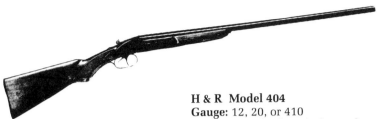

**Harrington & Richardson 404**

**H & R Model 404C**
Same as model 404 except: Monte
Carlo stock
Estimated Value: $150.00 - $200.00

**H & R Model 404**
**Gauge:** 12, 20, or 410
**Action:** Box lock; side lever, break-
open
**Magazine:** None
**Barrel:** Double barrel (side by side);
26" or 28"; variety of choke
combinations
**Finish:** Blued; checkered wood semi-
pistol grip stock & forearm
Estimated Value: $155.00 - $195.00

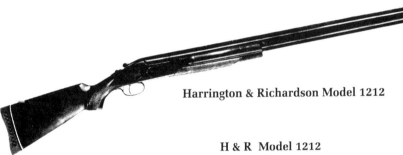

Harrington & Richardson Model 1212

**H & R Gamester 348**
**Gauge:** 12 or 16
**Action:** Bolt action; repeating
**Magazine:** 2-shot
**Barrel:** 28" full choke
**Finish:** Blued; plain wood, semi-
pistol grip stock & forearm
Estimated Value: $70.00 - $90.00

**H & R Model 1212**
**Gauge:** 12
**Action:** Box lock; top lever, break-
open; single selective trigger
**Magazine:** None
**Barrel:** Over & under double barrel;
28" improved modified over
improved cylinder; ventilated rib
**Finish:** Blued; decorated frame;
checkered walnut pistol grip stock &
forearm
Estimated Value: $270.00 - $335.00

**H & R Gamester 349 Deluxe**
Same as Gamester 348 except:
adjustable choke; 26" barrel; recoil
pad
Estimated Value: $ 80.00 - $100.00

**H & R Model 1212 Waterfowl**
Similar to the Model 1212 in 12
gauge magnum; 30" full choke over
modified barrel; ventilated recoil
pad
Estimated Value: $290.00 - $350.00

# Harrington & Richardson

**Harrington & Richardson Model 400**

**H & R  Huntsman 351**
**Gauge:** 12 or 16
**Action:** Bolt action; repeating
**Magazine:** 2-shot tubular
**Barrel:** 26"; adjustable choke
**Finish:** Blued; plain Monte Carlo semi-pistol grip stock & forearm; recoil pad
**Estimated Value: $75.00 - $95.00**

**H & R  Model 400**
**Gauge:** 12, 16, or 20
**Action:** Slide action; hammerless; repeating
**Magazine:** 5-shot tubular
**Barrel:** 28" full choke
**Finish:** Blued; semi-pistol grip stock & grooved slide handle
**Estimated Value: $130.00 - $160.00**

**Harrington & Richardson Model 402**

**H & R  Model 401**
Same as the 400 except: adjustable choke
**Estimated Value: $130.00 - $165.00**

**H& R  Model 402**
Similar to the model 400 except: 410 gauge only
**Estimated Value: $135.00 - $170.00**

**Harrington & Richardson 440**

**Harrington & Richardson 442**

**H & R  Model 442**
Similar to the model 440 except: ventilated rib & checkering
**Estimated Value: $145.00 - $180.00**

**H & R  Model 440**
**Gauge:** 12, 16, or 20
**Action:** Slide action; hammerless; repeating
**Magazine:** 4-shot clip
**Barrel:** 24", 26", or 28"; variety of chokes
**Finish:** Blued; walnut semi-pistol grip stock & forearm; recoil pad
**Estimated Value: $130.00 - $165.00**

**Harrington & Richardson 403**

**H & R Model 403**
**Gauge:** 410
**Action:** Semi-automatic
**Magazine:** 4-shot tubular
**Barrel:** 26" full choke
**Finish:** Blued; wood semi-pistol grip stock & fluted forearm
**Estimated Value: $175.00 - $225.00**

# High Standard

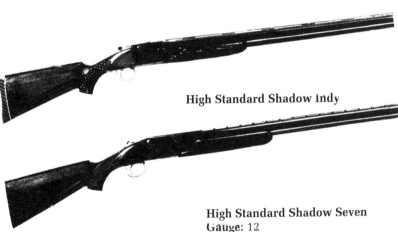

**High Standard Shadow Indy**

**High Standard Shadow Seven**

**High Standard Shadow Seven**
**Gauge:** 12
**Action:** Box lock; top lever, break-open; hammerless; single selective trigger; automatic ejectors
**Magazine:** None
**Barrel:** Over & under double barrel; 27½" or 29½"; variety of chokes; ventilated rib
**Finish:** Blued; checkered walnut pistol grip stock & forearm; gold plated trigger
**Estimated Value: $440.00 - $550.00**

**High Standard Shadow Indy**
Similar to Shadow Seven except: higher quality finish; chrome lined barrels; engraving
**Estimated Value: $540.00 - $675.00**

## High Standard

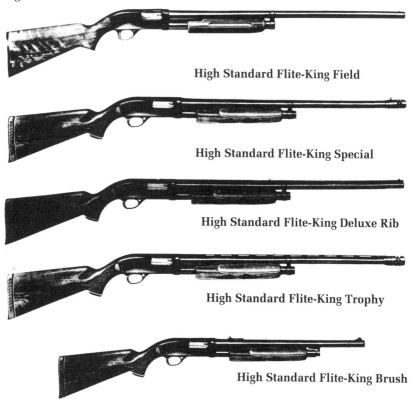

High Standard Flite-King Field

High Standard Flite-King Special

High Standard Flite-King Deluxe Rib

High Standard Flite-King Trophy

High Standard Flite-King Brush

**High Standard Flite-King Field**
**Gauge:** 12, 16, 20, or 410
**Action:** Slide action; hammerless; repeating
**Magazine:** 5-shot tubular; 4-shot tubular in 20 gauge
**Barrel:** 26" improved cylinder; 28" modified; 30" full choke
**Finish:** Blued; plain walnut semi-pistol grip stock & grooved slide handle
**Estimated Value: $130.00 - $165.00**

**High Standard Flite-King Special**
Similar to Flite-King Field except: adjustable choke & 27" barrel; no 410 gauge
**Estimated Value: $135.00 - $170.00**

**High Standard Flite-King Deluxe Rib**
Similar to the Flite-King Field except: ventilated rib & checkered wood
**Estimated Value: $145.00 - $180.00**

**High Standard Flite-King Trophy**
Similar to the Flight-King Deluxe Rib except: adjustable choke & 27" barrel; no 410 gauge
**Estimated Value: $150.00 - $190.00**

**High Standard Flite-King Brush**
Similar to Flite-King Field except: 18" or 20" cylinder bore barrel; rifle sights; 12 gauge only
**Estimated Value: $140.00 - $185.00**

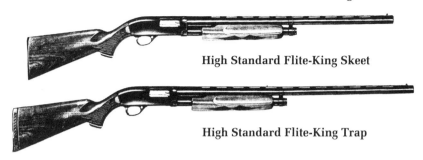

High Standard Flite-King Skeet

High Standard Flite-King Trap

**High Standard Flite-King Skeet**
Similar to the Flight-King Deluxe Rib except: skeet choke; 26" ventilated rib barrel; no 16 gauge
**Estimated Value: $155.00 - $195.00**

**High Standard Flite-King Trap**
Similar to the Flight-King Deluxe Rib except: 30" full choke barrel; trap stock; 26" barrel in 410 gauge
**Estimated Value: $155.00 - $195.00**

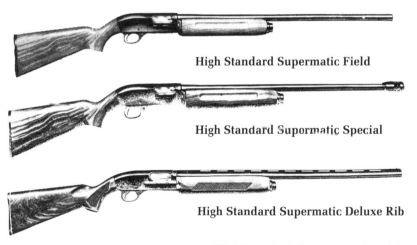

High Standard Supermatic Field

High Standard Supermatic Special

High Standard Supermatic Deluxe Rib

**High Standard Supermatic Special**
Similar to the Supermatic Field except: adjustable choke & 27" barrel
**Estimated Value: $185.00 - $230.00**

**High Standard Supermatic Field**
**Gauge:** 12 or 20; 20 magnum
**Action:** Semi-automatic, gas operated; hammerless
**Magazine:** 4-shot tubular; 3-shot tubular in 20 magnum
**Barrel:** 26", 28", or 30"; many chokes
**Finish:** Blued; plain walnut semi-pistol grip stock & fluted forearm
**Estimated Value: $175.00 - $220.00**

**High Standard Supermatic Deluxe Rib**
Similar to Supermatic Field except: 28" modified or full choke barrel, (30" in 12 gauge); checkered wood & ventilated rib
**Estimated Value: $190.00 - $235.00**

# High Standard

High Standard Supermatic Trophy

High Standard Supermatic Duck

High Standard Supermatic Trap

**High Standard Shadow Automatic**

**High Standard Supermatic Trophy**
Similar to the Supermatic Field with a 27" barrel; adjustable choke; ventilated rib; checkering
**Estimated Value: $200.00 - $250.00**

**High Standard Supermatic Skeet**
Similar to Supermatic Field Model except: 26" ventilated rib barrel; skeet choke; checkered wood
**Estimated Value: $210.00 - $260.00**

**High Standard Supermatic Duck**
Similar to the Supermatic Field except: 12 gauge magnum with a 30" full choke barrel & recoil pad
**Estimated Value: $190.00 - $240.00**

**High Standard Supermatic Duck Rib**
Similar to the Supermatic Duck except: checkered wood & ventilated rib
**Estimated Value: $200.00 - $250.00**

**High Standard Supermatic Trap**
Similar to the Supermatic Field in 12 gauge only; 30" full choke; ventilated rib; checkered trap stock & forearm; recoil pad
**Estimated Value: $200.00 - $245.00**

**High Standard Shadow Automatic**
**Gauge:** 12 or 20; regular or magnum
**Action:** Semi-automatic; gas operated; hammerless
**Magazine:** 4-shot tubular
**Barrel:** 26", 28", or 30"; variety of chokes; ventilated rib
**Finish:** Blued; walnut pistol grip stock & forearm
**Estimated Value: $210.00 - $260.00**

# Hunter

**Hunter Fulton**

**Hunter Fulton**
**Gauge:** 12, 16, or 20
**Action:** Box lock; top lever, break-open; hammerless; double or single trigger; add $50.00 for single trigger
**Magazine:** None
**Barrel:** Double barrel (side by side); 26", 28", 30", or 32"; various choke combinations
**Finish:** Blued; checkered walnut pistol grip stock & forearm
**Estimated Value: $400.00 - $500.00**

**Hunter Special**
Similar to Hunter Fulton except: higher quality; add $50.00 for single trigger
**Estimated Value: $490.00 - $650.00**

# Ithaca

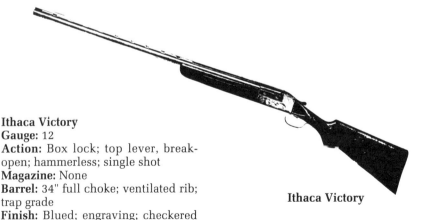

**Ithaca Victory**

**Ithaca Victory**
**Gauge:** 12
**Action:** Box lock; top lever, break-open; hammerless; single shot
**Magazine:** None
**Barrel:** 34" full choke; ventilated rib; trap grade
**Finish:** Blued; engraving; checkered pistol grip stock & forearm; made in five grades; estimated value is for standard grade
**Estimated Value: $825.00 - $1,100.00**

## Ithaca

**Ithaca Hammerless Double Field Grade**
**Gauge:** 12, 16, 20, 28, or 410
**Action:** Box lock; top lever, break-open; hammerless
**Magazine:** None
**Barrel:** Double barrel (side by side); 26", 28", 30", or 32"; various choke combinations
**Finish:** Blued; checkered walnut pistol grip stock & short tapered forearm; made in eight grades; Priced here for Standard Grade; add $50.00 for automatic ejectors, magnum or ventilated rib
**Estimated Value: $400.00 - $550.00**

**Ithaca Hammerless Double Field Grade**

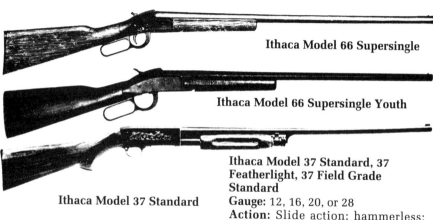

**Ithaca Model 66 Supersingle**

**Ithaca Model 66 Supersingle Youth**

**Ithaca Model 37 Standard**

**Ithaca Model 66 Supersingle**
**Gauge:** 20 or 410
**Action:** Lever action; exposed hammer; single shot
**Magazine:** None
**Barrel:** 26", 28", or 30"; full or modified choke
**Finish:** Blued; plain or checkered straight stock & forearm
**Estimated Value: $70.00 - $90.00**

**Ithaca Model 66 Supersingle Youth**
Similar to the 66 except: shorter stock; 410 gauge; 25" barrel; recoil pad
**Estimated Value: $65.00 - $85.00**

**Ithaca Model 37 Standard, 37 Featherlight, 37 Field Grade Standard**
**Gauge:** 12, 16, 20, or 28
**Action:** Slide action; hammerless; repeating; bottom ejection
**Magazine:** 4-shot tubular
**Barrel:** 26", 28", or 30" various chokes
**Finish:** Blued; walnut, semi-pistol grip stock & grooved or checkered slide handle; add 25% for magnum with interchangeable choke tubes
**Estimated Value: $185.00 - $250.00**

**Ithaca Model 37V, 37 Featherlight Vent, 37 Field Grade Vent**
Similar to the Model 37 except: ventilated rib; three interchangeable choke tubes
**Estimated Value: $240.00 - $320.00**

**Ithaca Model 37R**

**Ithaca Model 37D Deluxe**
Similar to the 37 except: checkered
stock & slide handle
Estimated Value: $200.00 - $260.00

**Ithaca Model 37R Deluxe**
Similar to the 37 Deluxe with a
raised solid rib
Estimated Value: $225.00 - $300.00

**Ithaca Model 37DV Deluxe Vent**
Similar to the 37D Deluxe except:
ventilated rib
Estimated Value: $310.00 - $390.00

**Ithaca Model 37T Trap**
Similar to the 37S with trap stock;
recoil pad; choice wood
Estimated Value: $230.00 - $300.00

**Ithaca Model 37R**
Similar to the 37 with a solid raised
rib; slightly heavier
Estimated Value: $220.00 - $275.00

**Ithaca Model 37 Supreme,
37 Featherlight Supreme,**
Similar to the 37T Target
Estimated Value: $490.00 - $615.00

**Ithaca Model 37 Deerslayer**

**Ithaca Model 37S Skeet**
Similar to the 37 with extended
slide handle & ventilated rib
Estimated Value: $225.00 - $300.00

**Ithaca Model 37 Deerslayer**
Similar to the Model 37 except: 20"
or 25" barrel; rifle sights; 12 or 20
gauge
Estimated Value: $255.00 - $320.00

**Ithaca Model 37T Target**
Available in skeet or trap version
with high-quality finish & select
wood. Replaced the 37S & 37T Trap
Estimated Value: $245.00 - $325.00

**Ithaca Model 37
Deerslayer Super Deluxe**
Similar to the Model 37 Deerslayer
with higher quality wood & finish
Estimated Value: $275.00 - $350.00

# Ithaca

Ithaca Model 37 M&P

## Ithaca Model 37 M&P, 87 M&P
Similar to the Model 37 except: for law enforcement use; 18" or 20" cylinder bore barrel; non-glare tung oil finish wood; parkerized or chrome finish metal; add 10% for chrome ; 5 or 8-shot magazine; add 7% for hand grip
Estimated Value: $200.00 - $250.00

## Ithaca Model 37 DSPS, DSPS II
A law enforcement version of the Model 37 Deerslayer; grooved slide handle; regular, parkerized, or chrome finished; add 15% for chrome finish; add 5% for 8-shot magazine; deduct 5% for DSPS II
Estimated Value: $200.00 - $250.00

## Ithaca Bear Stopper
A short barrel version of the Model 37; 18½" or 20" barrel; 12 gauge; one-hand grip; grooved slide handle; 5 or 8-shot magazine; add 5% for 8-shot; blued or chrome finish; add 10% for chrome
Estimated Value: $225.00 - $300.00

## Ithaca Model 37 Ultra Deerslayer,
Similar to the Ultra Featherlight except: 20" barrel for slugs; sights; recoil pad; swivels
Estimated Value: $250.00 - $315.00

## Ithaca Model 37 Camo Vent
Similar to the Model 37 Field Grade Vent except: rust-resistant camo finish in spring (green) or fall (brown); sling & swivels; 12 gauge; 26" or 28" full choke barrel
Estimated Value: $330.00 - $410.00

Ithaca Model 37 Ultra Featherlight

## Ithaca Model 37 English-Ultra Featherlight
Gauge: 12 or 20
Action: Slide action; hammerless; repeating; aluminum receiver
Magazine: 3-shot tubular
Barrel: 25" full, modified or improved cylinder bore; ventilated rib
Finish: Blued; checkered walnut straight grip stock & slide handle; waterfowl scene on receiver
Estimated Value: $290.00 - $365.00

## Ithaca Model 37 Basic Featherlight
Similar to the Model 37 except: without cosmetic finish; no checkering; wood finished in non-glare tung oil; grooved slide handle; "vapor blasted" metal surfaces with a non-glare finish; add 2% for ventilated rib; add 30% for magnum
Estimated Value: $200.00 - $260.00

## Ithaca Model 37 & 87 Ultra Featherlight
A 20 gauge lightweight version of the Model 37; aluminum receiver; 25" barrel with ventilated rib; recoil pad; gold plated trigger; interchangeable choke tubes on model 87
Estimated Value: $260.00 - $320.00

Ithaca Model 87 Field

**Ithaca Model 87 Ultra Field**
Same as Model 87 Field except: aluminum receiver
**Estimated Value: $260.00 - $320.00**

**Ithaca Model 87 Field**
**Gauge:** 12 or 20
**Action:** Slide action; hammerless; repeating
**Magazine:** 3-shot tubular
**Barrel:** 26", 28", or 30"; three choke tubes; 3" chamber; ventilated rib
**Finish:** Blued; pressed checkered American walnut stock & side handle
**Estimated Value: $275.00 - $345.00**

**Ithaca Model 87 Camo Field**
Same as Model 87 Field except: 12 gauge with 28" barrel; smooth American walnut stock & grooved slide handle; camouflaged finish
**Estimated Value: $315.00 - $395.00**

**Ithaca Model 87 M&P & 87DSPS**
Same as Model 87 Field except: 12 gauge with 20" plain barrel; dull oil finished wood; parkerized or nickel finish metal; add 25% for nickel finish; 5 or 8-shot magazine; cylinder choke
**Estimated Value: $245.00 - $300.00**

**Ithaca Model 87 Deluxe**
Same as Model 87 Field except: cut checkered stock & slide handle with a high gloss finish & gold plated trigger
**Estimated Value: $300.00 - $370.00**

**Ithaca Model 87 Supreme**
Same as Model 87 Field except: high grade finish & checkering; gold plated trigger; Raybar irridescent orange front sight
**Estimated Value: $490.00 - $610.00**

**Ithaca Model 87 Turkey**
Same as Model 87 Field except: 12 gauge with 24" barrel; smooth stock & slide handle;  full choke barrel or full choke tube; matte blue barrel with oil finished wood or camouflaged finish; add $10.00 for extra choke tube; add 25% for camouflaged finish
**Estimated Value:  $250.00 - $315.00**

# Ithaca

**Ithaca Model 87 Deerslayer II**

## Ithaca Model English 87
Same as model 37 English Ultra Featherlight except: 20 gauge only; 24" or 26" barrel; 3 changeable choke tubes; steel receiver
Estimated Value: $295.00 - $370.00

## Ithaca Model 87 Deerslayer
Same as Model 87 Field except: 20" or 25" special bore plain barrel for rifled slugs; 12 gauge only; smooth oil finished stock & grooved slide handle; plain matte finished barrel
Estimated Value: $235.00 - $290.00

## Ithaca Model 87 Deerslayer II
Same as Model 87 Deluxe Deerslayer except: Monte Carlo stock; rifled barrel is permanently screwed into the receiver.
Estimated Value: $315.00 - $390.00

## Ithaca Model 87 Deluxe Deerslayer
Same as Model 87 Field except: 20" or 25" barrel; cut checkering with high gloss finish; plain barrel with Raybar front sight & adjustable rear; gold plated trigger; special bore; slug barrel or rifled barrel; add 8% for rifled barrel
Estimated Value: $255.00 - $320.00

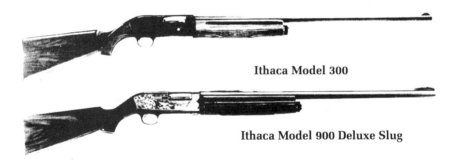

**Ithaca Model 300**

**Ithaca Model 900 Deluxe Slug**

## Ithaca Model 300
**Gauge:** 12 or 20
**Action:** Semi-automatic; recoil operated; hammerless
**Magazine:** 3-shot tubular
**Barrel:** 26" improved cylinder; 28" modified or full, 30" full choke; ventilated rib optional; add $10.00 for ventilated rib
**Finish:** Blued; checkered walnut pistol grip stock & forearm
Estimated Value: $200.00 - $250.00

## Ithaca Model 900 Deluxe
Similar to the 300 except: ventilated rib; gold-filled engraving; nameplate in stock; gold-plated trigger
Estimated Value: $240.00 - $300.00

## Ithaca Model 900 Deluxe Slug
Similar to the 900 Deluxe except: 24" barrel for slugs; rifle sights
Estimated Value: $245.00 - $310.00

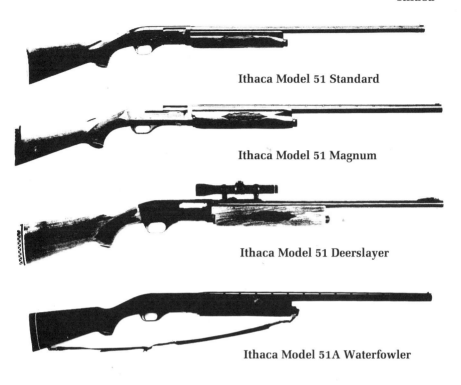

Ithaca Model 51 Standard

Ithaca Model 51 Magnum

Ithaca Model 51 Deerslayer

Ithaca Model 51A Waterfowler

**Ithaca Model 51 Standard,
51 Featherlight, 51A**
**Gauge:** 12 or 20
**Action:** Gas operated, semi-automatic
**Magazine:** 3-shot tubular
**Barrel:** 26", 28", or 30"; various chokes; ventilated rib optional; add 5% for ventilated rib
**Finish:** Blued; checkered walnut pistol grip stock & forearm; decorated receiver
**Estimated Value: $260.00 - $350.00**

**Ithaca Model 51 Magnum**
Similar to the 51 but chambered for magnum shells; ventilated rib
**Estimated Value: $310.00 - $390.00**

**Ithaca Model 51 Deerslayer**
Similar to the Model 51 except: 24" barrel for slugs; sights; recoil pad; 12 gauge only
**Estimated Value: $260.00 - $350.00**

**Ithaca Model 51A Waterfowler, 51A
Turkey Gun**
Similar to the Model 51A except: matte-finish metal & flat-finish walnut; optional camo finish; add 10% for camo finish; The Turkey model has a 26" ventilated rib barrel, the Waterfowler has a 30" ventilated rib barrel.
**Estimated Value: $350.00 - $465.00**

# Ithaca

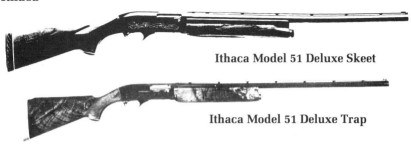

Ithaca Model 51 Deluxe Skeet

Ithaca Model 51 Deluxe Trap

**Ithaca Model 51 Deluxe Skeet, 51A Supreme Skeet**
Similar to the 51 with recoil pad; ventilated rib; 26", 28", or 29" skeet choke barrel
Estimated Value: $480.00 - $645.00

**Ithaca Model 51 Deluxe Trap, 51A Supreme Trap**
Similar to the Model 51 except: 12 gauge only; select wood; 28" or 30" barrel; recoil pad; add 5% for Monte Carlo stock
Estimated Value: $490.00 - $650.00

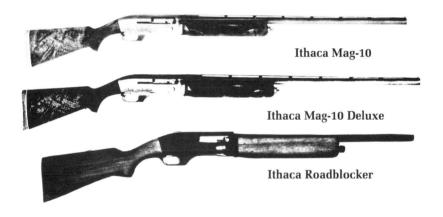

Ithaca Mag-10

Ithaca Mag-10 Deluxe

Ithaca Roadblocker

**Ithaca Mag-10 Standard or Deluxe**
**Gauge:** 10 magnum
**Action:** Semi-automatic; gas operated
**Magazine:** 3-shot tubular
**Barrel:** 32" full choke; ventilated rib (deluxe model)
**Finish:** Blued; plain (standard model) or checkered walnut pistol grip stock & forearm; recoil pad; swivels; deduct 15% for Ithaca Mag-10 Standard
Estimated Value: $525.00 - $700.00

**Ithaca Mag-10 Supreme**
Similar to the Magnum 10 Deluxe with higher quality finish & select wood
Estimated Value: $630.00 - $840.00

**Ithaca Mag-10 Roadblocker**
A law enforcement version of the Mag-10 with a 20" barrel; plain stock & forearm; "vapor blasted" metal finish; add 5% for ventilated rib
Estimated Value: $420.00 - $560.00

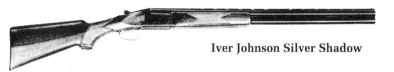

Iver Johnson Silver Shadow

**Iver Johnson Super Trap**

**Iver Johnson Super Trap**
**Gauge:** 12
**Action:** Box lock; top lever, break-open; hammerless; non-selective or selective single trigger or automatic ejectors optional; add $35.00 for non-selective single trigger; $75.00 for selective single trigger or automatic ejectors
**Magazine:** None
**Barrel:** Double barrel (side by side); 32" full choke; ventilated rib
**Finish:** Blued; checkered walnut pistol grip stock & forearm; recoil pad
**Estimated Value:** $450.00 - $575.00

**Johnson Silver Shadow**
**ge:** 12
**on:** Box lock; top lever, break-n; hammerless; single trigger nal; add $75.00 for single trigger
**azine:** None
**el:** Over & under double barrel; nodified & full choke; ventilated

**sh:** Blued; checkered walnut l grip stock & forearm
**ated Value:** $300.00 - $375.00

## ssler

**er Lever Matic**
**ge:** 12, 16, or 20
**on:** Lever action
**azine:** 3-shot
**el:** 26", 28", or 30"; full choke
**sh:** Blued; checkered walnut ht stock & forearm; recoil pad
**ated Value:** $150.00 - $185.00

**Kessler 3-Shot**
**Gauge:** 12, 16, or 20
**Action:** Bolt action; hammerless; repeating
**Magazine:** 2-shot detachable box
**Barrel:** 26" or 28"; full choke
**Finish:** Blued; plain pistol grip stock & forearm, recoil pad
**Estimated Value:** $75.00 - $95.00

# Iver

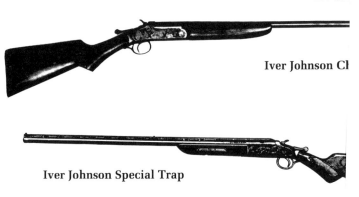

Iver Johnson Cl

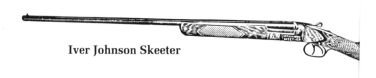

Iver Johnson Special Trap

Iver Johnson Skeeter

## Iver Johnson Champion
**Gauge:** 12, 20, or 410
**Action:** Box lock; top lever, break-open; hammerless; single shot; automatic ejector
**Magazine:** None
**Barrel:** 26", 28", or 30"; full choke
**Finish:** Blued; hardwood semi-pistol grip stock & short tapered forearm
**Estimated Value:** $85.00 - $110.00

## Iver Johnson Special Trap
Similar to the Champion with a 32" ribbed barrel; checkered stock; 12 gauge only
**Estimated Value:** $150.00 - $190.00

## Iver Johnson Matted Rib
Similar to the Champion with a matted rib & checkering
**Estimated Value:** $110.00 - $135.00

## Iver Johnson Hercule:
**Gauge:** 12, 16, 20, or ‹
**Action:** Box lock; to open; hammerless; s automatic ejectors $75.00 for single trigg ejectors
**Magazine:** None
**Barrel:** Double barrel 26", 28", 30", or 32" or full & full chokes
**Finish:** Blued; che pistol grip stock & tar
**Estimated Value:** $320

## Iver Johnson Skeetei
Similar to the F addition of 28 gat barrels; wide forea for single select: automatic ejectors
**Estimated Value:** $40

Ive
Ga
Ac
op
opt
Ma
Bar
28"
rib
Fin
pist
Esti

## Ke

Kes
Ga
Act
Ma
Bar
Fin
stra
Esti

# Kleinguenther

Kleinguenther Condor

**Kleinguenther Condor Skeet**
A skeet version of the Condor with a wide rib
**Estimated Value: $500.00 - $625.00**

**Kleinguenther Condor Trap**
A trap version of the Condor with a Monte Carlo stock; wide rib; 32" barrel available
**Estimated Value: $510.00 - $640.00**

**Kleinguenther Condor**
**Gauge:** 12 or 20
**Action:** Double lock; top lever break-open; hammerless; selective single trigger; automatic ejectors
**Magazine:** None
**Barrel:** Over & under double barrel; ventilated rib; 26" improved & modified or skeet; 28" modified or modified & full; 30" modified & full or full in 12 gauge
**Finish:** Blued; checkered walnut pistol grip stock & forearm; recoil pad
**Estimated Value: $480.00 - $600.00**

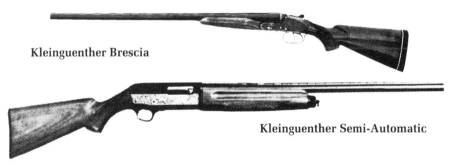

Kleinguenther Brescia

Kleinguenther Semi-Automatic

**Kleinguenther Brescia**
**Gauge:** 12 or 20
**Action:** Box lock; top lever, break-open; hammerless; double trigger
**Magazine:** None
**Barrel:** Double barrel (side by side); chrome lined; 28" improved or modified or modified & full chokes
**Finish:** Blued; checkered walnut pistol grip stock & tapered forearm
**Estimated Value: $240.00 - $300.00**

**Kleinguenther Semi-Automatic**
**Gauge:** 12
**Action:** Semi-auto; hammerless; side ejection
**Magazine:** 3-shot tubular
**Barrel:** Chrome lined; 25" skeet, 26" improved cylinder, 28" & 30" full chokes; ventilated rib
**Finish:** Blued; smooth walnut pistol grip stock & grooved forearm; engraved
**Estimated Value: $260.00 - $325.00**

# L.C. Smith

L.C. Smith Double Barrel
(Hunter Arms)

### L.C. Smith Single Barrel
**Gauge:** 12
**Action:** Box lock; top lever, break-open; automatic ejectors; hammerless
**Magazine:** None, single shot
**Barrel:** 32" or 34"; choice of bore; ventilated rib
**Finish:** Blued; checkered walnut pistol grip stock & forearm; recoil pad
**Estimated Value:**
    Olympic: $1,050.00 - $1,500.00
    Specialty: $1,450.00 - $2,000.00
    Crown: $2,500.00 - $3,200.00

### L.C. Smith Double Barrel (Hunter Arms)
**Gauge:** 12, 16, 20, or 410
**Action:** Side lock, top lever break-down; hammerless; automatic ejectors; double or single trigger; add $50.00 for single trigger
**Magazine:** None
**Barrel:** 26", 28", 30", or 32"; double barrel (side by side) any choke combination
**Finish:** checkered walnut pistol, semi-pistol grip or straight grip stock & forearm; blued barrels; prices are for Field Grade made by Hunter Arms; other grades higher due to quality of workmanship & finish
**Estimated Value:** $650.00 - $800.00

L.C. Smith Field Grade (Marlin)

### L.C. Smith Field Grade (Marlin)
Same as the Deluxe Model with standard checkered walnut pistol grip stock & forearm; extruded ventilated rib
**Estimated Value:** $400.00 - $500.00

### L.C. Smith Deluxe (Marlin)
**Gauge:** 12, regular or magnum
**Action:** Top lever break-open; hammerless; side lock; double triggers
**Magazine:** None
**Barrel:** Double barrel (side by side); 28" modified & full chokes; floating steel ventilated rib
**Finish:** Top quality, hand-fitted, hand-checkered walnut pistol grip stock & beavertail forearm; blued; case hardened side plates
**Estimated Value:** $415.00 - $520.00

**Lefever Long Range**

**Lefever Long Range**
**Gauge:** 12, 16, 20, or 410
**Action:** Box lock, top lever, break-open; hammerless; single shot
**Magazine:** None
**Barrel:** 26", 28", 30", or 32"; any choke
**Finish:** Blued; plain or checkered walnut pistol grip stock & forearm
**Estimated Value:** $180.00 - $225.00

**Lefever Trap**
**Gauge:** 12
**Action:** Box lock; top lever break-open; hammerless; single shot
**Magazine:** None
**Barrel:** 30" or 32" full choke; ventilated rib
**Finish:** Blued; checkered walnut pistol grip stock & forearm; recoil pad
**Estimated Value:** $360.00 - $450.00

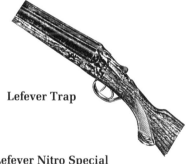

**Lefever Trap**

**Lefever Nitro Special**

**Lefever Excellsior**
Similar to Nitro-Special with light engraving & automatic ejectors
**Estimated Value:** $460.00 - $575.00

**Lefever Nitro Special**
**Gauge:** 12, 16, 20, or 410
**Action:** Box lock; top lever, break-open; hammerless; double triggers; single trigger optional; add $75.00 for single trigger
**Magazine:** None
**Barrel:** Double barrel (side by side); 26", 28", 30", or 32"; any choke
**Finish:** Blued; checkered walnut pistol grip stock & forearm
**Estimated Value:** $440.00 - $550.00

# Mannlicher

Mannlicher Gamba Oxford

## Mannlicher Gamba Oxford
**Gauge:** 12, 20, or 20; regular or magnum
**Action:** Top lever break-open; hammerless; single or double trigger; add $140.00 for single trigger
**Magazine:** None
**Barrel:** Double barrel (side by side); 26½" improved cylinder & modified or 27½" modified & full
**Finish:** Blued; engraved receiver; checkered walnut straight grip stock & tapered forearm
**Estimated Value: $995.00 - $1,325.00**

## Mannlicher Gamba Principessa
**Gauge:** 28
**Action:** Top lever break-open; hammerless; single or double trigger; add $130.00 for single trigger
**Magazine:** None
**Barrel:** Double barrel (side by side); 26" improved cylinder & modified or 28" modified & full
**Finish:** Blued; case hardened receiver with engraved scrollwork; checkered walnut straight grip stock & tapered forearm
**Estimated Value: $880.00 - $1,175.00**

# Marlin

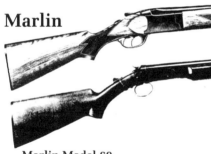

Marlin Model 90

Marlin Model 60

## Marlin Model 60
**Gauge:** 12
**Action:** Box lock; top lever, break-open; exposed hammer; single shot
**Magazine:** None
**Barrel:** 30" or 32" full choke; matted top; 2¾" chamber
**Finish:** Blued; walnut pistol grip stock & beavertail forearm
**Estimated Value: $145.00 - $185.00**

## Marlin Model 90
**Gauge:** 12, 16, 20, or 410; add $40.00 for 410 gauge; also .22 & .222 calibers
**Action:** Top lever break-open; box lock; double trigger; single trigger optional; add $50.00 for single trigger; hammerless
**Magazine:** None
**Barrel:** Over & under double barrel, 26", 28", or 30" rifle; 26" shotgun barrels; 2¾" chamber, 3" chamber in 410; full, modified, skeet or improved cylinder bore
**Finish:** Blued; plain or checkered walnut pistol grip stock & forearm; recoil pad
**Estimated Value: $350.00 - $440.00**

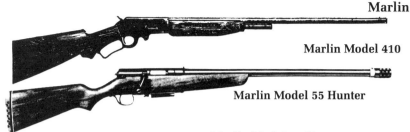

Marlin Model 410

Marlin Model 55 Hunter

**Marlin Model 410**
**Gauge:** 410
**Action:** Lever action; exposed hammer
**Magazine:** 5-shot tubular
**Barrel:** 22" or 26", 2½" chamber
**Finish:** Blued; walnut pistol grip stock & beavertail forearm
**Estimated Value: $375.00 - $470.00**

**Marlin Model 55 Hunter**
**Gauge:** 12, 16, or 20
**Action:** Bolt action; repeating
**Magazine:** 2-shot clip
**Barrel:** 26" or 28" full choke; also "Micro Choke;" 2¾" or 3" chamber
**Finish:** Blued; walnut pistol grip stock & forearm
**Estimated Value: $80.00 - $100.00**

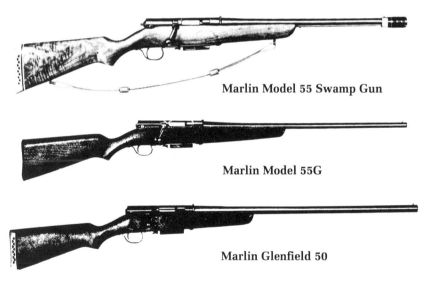

Marlin Model 55 Swamp Gun

Marlin Model 55G

Marlin Glenfield 50

**Marlin Model 55 Swamp Gun**
Same as the Model 55 except: shorter barrel with "Micro Choke;" recoil pad & swivels; chambered for 3" 12 gauge magnum shells
**Estimated Value: $80.00 - $100.00**

**Marlin 55G, Glenfield 55G & Glenfield 50**
Similar to the Marlin Model 55 Hunter; it was produced from about 1961 to 1966 as the 55G & Glenfield 55G, & in 1966 it became the Glenfield 50.
**Estimated Value: $75.00 - $95.00**

# Marlin

Marlin Model 55S Slug Gun

Marlin Model 55 Goose Gun

Marlin Model 59

Marlin Glenfield 60G

**Marlin Model 59, 60G, 61G**
**Gauge:** 410
**Action:** Bolt action
**Magazine:** None; single shot
**Barrel:** 24" full coke; chambered for 2½" or 3" shells
**Finish:** Blued; walnut pistol grip or semi-pistol grip stock & forearm
**Estimated Value: $70.00 - $90.00**

**Marlin Model 55S Slug Gun**
Similar to the Model 55 except: rifle sights; 24" barrel; chambered for 2¾" & 3" shells; swivels & recoil pad
**Estimated Value: $75.00 - $100.00**

**Marlin Model 55 Goose Gun**
Same as the Model 55 except: swivels; extra long 36" barrel; chambered for 3" 12 gauge magnum shells; recoil pad
**Estimated Value: $160.00 - $200.00**

**Marlin Model 5510 Supergoose 10**
**Gauge:** 10 gauge magnum
**Action:** Bolt action
**Magazine:** 2-shot clip (2⅞" shells must be loaded singly)
**Barrel:** 34" full choke; chambered for 3½" shells
**Finish:** Blued; black walnut semi-pistol grip stock & forearm; swivels; recoil pad
**Estimated Value: $165.00 - $210.00**

**Marlin Model 19**

**Marlin Model 1898**

**Marlin Model 1898**
**Gauge:** 12 (2¾")
**Action:** Slide action; exposed hammer; side ejection
**Magazine:** 5-shot tubular
**Barrel:** 26", 28", 30", or 32"
**Finish:** Blued; walnut pistol grip stock & grooved slide handle; produced in many grades from 1898 to 1905; price for Grade A (Field Grade)
**Estimated Value: $315.00 - $390.00**

**Marlin Model 19 & 19G**
Similar to the Model 1898 with improvements; Model 19 made from 1906 to 1907; 19G produced until 1915
**Estimated Value: $260.00 - $325.00**

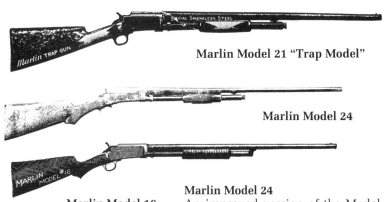

**Marlin Model 21 "Trap Model"**

**Marlin Model 24**

**Marlin Model 16**

**Marlin Model 24**
An improved version of the Model 19 made from 1908 to 1915
**Estimated Value: $270.00 - $355.00**

**Marlin Model 21 "Trap Model"**
Similar to the Model 24 with trap specifications. Made from 1907 to 1909
**Estimated Value: $275.00 - $345.00**

**Marlin Model 16**
**Gauge:** 16 (2¾")
**Action:** Slide action; exposed hammer
**Magazine:** 5-shot tubular
**Barrel:** 26" or 28"
**Finish:** Blued; walnut pistol grip stock & forearm; some checkered, some with grooved slide handle
**Estimated Value: $280.00 - $355.00**

**Marlin Model 26**
Similar to the Model 24 except: straight grip stock; solid frame
**Estimated Value: $260.00 - $325.00**

# Marlin

Marlin Model 28

Marlin Model 28T

Marlin Model 28A

Marlin Model 31

Marlin Model 31A

**Marlin Model 28, 28T, 28TS**
**Gauge:** 12
**Action:** Slide action; hammerless; side ejection
**Magazine:** 5-shot tubular
**Barrel:** 26" or 28" cylinder bore or modified choke; 30" or 32" full choke
**Finish:** Blued; checkered walnut pistol grip stock & slide handle; the Models 28T & 28TS were Trap Grade guns with an available straight stock; add $100.00 for 28T or 28TS
**Estimated Value: $280.00 - $350.00**

**Marlin Model 28A**
Similar to the Model 28; made from about 1920 to 1922; replaced by the Model 43A
**Estimated Value: $265.00 - $330.00**

**Marlin Model 31**
Similar to the Model 28 except: 20 or 16 gauge; made from about 1915 to 1917 & 1920 to 1922
**Estimated Value: $270.00 - $360.00**

**Marlin Model 31A**
Similar to the Model 28A except: 20 gauge only; replaced by the Model 44A
**Estimated Value: $265.00 - $350.00**

*Pocket Guide to Shotguns*

Marlin Model 30

## Marlin Model 17 & 17G
**Gauge:** 12
**Action:** Slide action; exposed hammer
**Magazine:** 5-shot tubular
**Barrel:** 30" or 32" full choke; other chokes available by special order
**Finish:** Blued; walnut pistol grip stock & grooved slide handle; after 1908 as Model 17G
**Estimated Value:** $265.00 - $330.00

## Marlin Model 30 & 30G
**Gauge:** 16 or 20
**Action:** Slide action; exposed hammer
**Magazine:** 5-shot tubular
**Barrel:** 25", 26", or 28" modified choke, 2¾" chamber
**Finish:** Blued; checkered walnut straight or pistol grip stock, grooved or checkered slide handle; after 1915 it was called the Model 30G
**Estimated Value:** $235.00 - $295.00

Marlin Model 42A

## Marlin Model 49
Similar to the Model 42A. It was given away with stock in the corporation. Produced from about 1925 to 1928
**Estimated Value:** $275.00 - $375.00

## Marlin Model 42A
**Gauge:** 12
**Action:** Slide action; exposed hammer; side ejection
**Magazine:** 5-shot tubular; bottom load
**Barrel:** 26" cylinder bore, 28" modified, 30" & 32" full choke; 2¾" chamber; round matted barrel
**Finish:** Blued; black walnut semi-pistol grip stock; grooved slide handle
**Estimated Value:** $230.00 - $290.00

# Marlin

Marlin Model 43A

Marlin Model 43T

Marlin Model 44A

## Marlin Model 43A
**Gauge:** 12
**Action:** Slide action; hammerless; side ejection
**Magazine:** 5-shot tubular
**Barrel:** 26" cylinder bore, 28" modified, 30" & 32" full choke; 2¾" chamber
**Finish:** Blued; walnut pistol grip stock & grooved slide handle
**Estimated Value: $200.00 - $250.00**

## Marlin Model 43T & 43TS
Same basic shotgun as the Model 43A except: checkered Monte Carlo stock & forearm with recoil pad; the Model 43TS had a choice of many options, & the value is dependent on the number & type of extras.
**Estimated Value: $300.00 - $375.00**

## Marlin Model 53
Similar to Model 43A; made in Standard Grade only; replaced by Model 63A
**Estimated Value: $280.00 - $350.00**

## Marlin Model 44A
**Gauge:** 20
**Action:** Slide action; hammerless; side ejection
**Magazine:** 4-shot tubular; bottom load
**Barrel:** 25" or 28"; cylinder bore, modified or full choke; 2¾" chamber
**Finish:** Blued; walnut pistol grip stock & grooved slide handle
**Estimated Value: $285.00 - $360.00**

## Marlin Model 44S
Same basic shotgun as the Model 44A except: straight or pistol grip checkered stock & forearm
**Estimated Value: $295.00 - $370.00**

**Marlin Model 63A**
**Gauge:** 12
**Action:** Slide action; hammerless; side ejector
**Magazine:** 5-shot tubular
**Barrel:** 26" cylinder bore, 28" modified choke, 30" or 32" full choke
**Finish:** Blued; plain walnut pistol grip stock & grooved slide handle; improved version of the Model 43A
**Estimated Value: $200.00 - $275.00**

**Marlin Model 63T & 63TS**
Similar to the Model 63A except: trap version; 30" or 32" barrel; checkered straight stock; the Model 63TS could be ordered to the buyer's specifications; prices are for Standard Trap gun
**Estimated Value: $240.00 - $325.00**

Marlin Model Premier Mark I

Marlin Model Premier Mark II

Marlin Model Premier Mark IV

**Marlin Model Premier Mark I**
**Gauge:** 12
**Action:** Slide action; hammerless; side ejection
**Magazine:** 3-shot tubular
**Barrel:** 26" cylinder bore, 28" modified, 30" full choke; ventilated rib optional; also 28" slug barrel with rifle sights; 2¾" chamber
**Finish:** Blued; walnut pistol grip stock & forearm; recoil pad optional
**Estimated Value: $135.00 - $170.00**

**Marlin Model Premier Mark II**
Same as the Premier Mark I except: stock & forearm are checkered & receiver is engraved
**Estimated Value: $165.00 - $210.00**

**Marlin Model Premier Mark IV**
Same as the Mark II except: the wood is more elaborate & the engraving heavier
**Estimated Value: $230.00 - $290.00**

# Marlin

Marlin Model 120 Magnum

Marlin Model 120T

**Marlin Deluxe 120 Slug Gun**
Similar to the Marlin 120 except: 20"
slug barrel & rifle sights
**Estimated Value: $230.00 - $290.00**

**Marlin Model 120T**
Same as Model 120 with a Monte
Carlo stock & 30" full choke or 30"
modified trap choke barrel
**Estimated Value: $240.00 - $300.00**

**Marlin Model 120 Magnum**
**Gauge:** 12 gauge magnum
**Action:** Slide action; hammerless
**Magazine:** 5-shot tubular (4-shot
with 3" shells)
**Barrel:** 26" cylinder bore, 28"
modified or 30" full choke; also 26"
choked slug barrel
**Finish:** Blued; ventilated rib;
checkered walnut, pistol grip stock
& forearm; recoil pad
**Estimated Value: $225.00 - $280.00**

Marlin Glenfield 778

**Marlin Glenfield 778**
**Gauge:** 12, regular or magnum
**Action:** Slide action; hammerless;
repeating
**Magazine:** 5-shot tubular; 4-shot for
3" magnum
**Barrel:** 26" improved cylinder; 28"
modified; 30" full choke; ventilated
rib optional; add $50.00 for
ventilated rib; 38" MXR full choke
barrel available without rib
**Finish:** Blued; checkered hardwood,
semi-pistol grip stock & fluted slide
handle; recoil pad
**Estimated Value: $145.00 - $180.00**

**Marlin Glenfield 778 Slug**
Same as the Glenfield 778 except:
20" slug barrel & rifle sights
**Estimated Value: $150.00 - $200.00**

# Mauser

**Mauser Model 496 Trap**

**Mauser Model 496 Competition**

**Mauser Model 496 Competition**
Same as the Model 496 except: select wood; higher ventilated rib
**Estimated Value: $540.00 - $675.00**

**Mauser Model 496 Trap**
**Gauge:** 12
**Action:** Box lock; top lever, break-open; hammerless; single shot
**Magazine:** None
**Barrel:** 32" modified or 34" full choke; ventilated rib
**Finish:** Blued; checkered walnut Monte Carlo pistol grip stock & tapered forearm; engraved; recoil pad
**Estimated Value: $440.00 - $550.00**

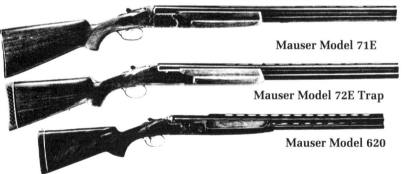

**Mauser Model 71E**

**Mauser Model 72E Trap**

**Mauser Model 620**

**Mauser Model 71E**
Similar to the Model 620 except: double triggers & no recoil pad; 28" barrel
**Estimated Value: $380.00 - $475.00**

**Mauser Model 72E Trap**
Similar to the Model 71E except: large recoil pad; engraving; wide high rib; single trigger
**Estimated Value: $500.00 - $625.00**

**Mauser Model 620**
**Gauge:** 12
**Action:** Box lock; top lever, break-open; hammerless; automatic ejectors; single trigger
**Magazine:** None
**Barrel:** Over & under double barrel; 28" or 30" improved cylinder & modified or modified & full or skeet chokes; ventilated rib
**Finish:** Blued; plain walnut pistol grip stock & forearm; recoil pad
**Estimated Value: $760.00 - $950.00**

# Mauser

**Mauser Model 580**

**Mauser Model 580**
**Gauge:** 12
**Action:** Side lock; top lever break-open; hammerless
**Magazine:** None
**Barrel:** Double barrel (side by side); 28" or 30", various choke combinations
**Finish:** Blued; checkered walnut straight stock & tapered forearm; engraved
**Estimated Value: $720.00 - $900.00**

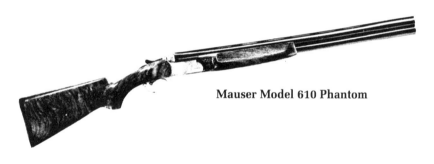

**Mauser Model 610 Phantom**

**Mauser Model 610 Phantom**
**Gauge:** 12
**Action:** Box lock; top lever, break-open; hammerless
**Magazine:** None
**Barrel:** Over & under double barrel; ventilated rib between barrels & on top of barrel; 30" or 32" various choke combinations
**Finish:** Blued; case hardened receiver; checkered walnut pistol grip stock & forearm; recoil pad
**Estimated Value: $780.00 - $975.00**

**Mauser Contest**
**Gauge:** 12
**Action:** Top lever, break-open; automatic ejectors; single selective trigger
**Magazine:** None
**Barrel:** Over & under double barrel; 27½" improved cylinder & improved modified
**Finish:** Blued; engraved gray sideplates; checkered walnut pistol grip stock & lipped forearm
**Estimated Value: 840.00 - $1,050.00**

# Mossberg

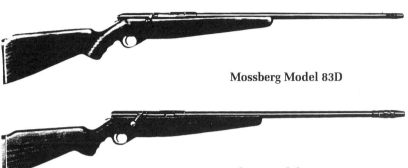

Mossberg Model 83D

Mossberg Model 183K

**Mossberg Model 83D, 183D**
**Gauge:** 410
**Action:** Bolt action; repeating
**Magazine:** 2-shot, top loading, fixed magazine
**Barrel:** 23" on 83D, 24" on 183D; interchangeable choke fittings
**Finish:** Blued; hardwood Monte Carlo semi-pistol grip one-piece stock & forearm; after 1948 called 183D
**Estimated Value: $75.00 - $95.00**

**Mossberg Model 183K**
Same as183D except: adjustable choke & recoil pad
**Estimated Value: $80.00 - $110.00**

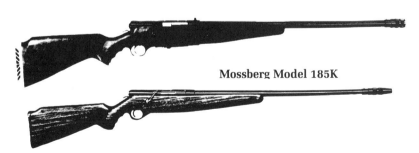

Mossberg Model 185K

Mossberg Model 190K

**Mossberg Model 190K**
Same as 183K except: 16 gauge
**Estimated Value: $75.00 - $95.00**

**Mossberg Model 185K**
Same as 183K except: 20 gauge
**Estimated Value: $80.00 - $100.00**

**Mossberg Model 195K**
Same as 183K except: 12 gauge
**Estimated Value: $85.00 - $105.00**

# Mossberg

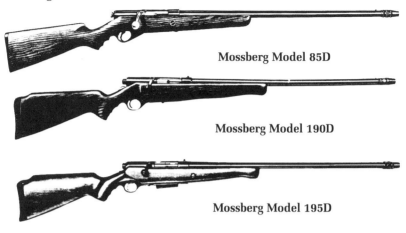

Mossberg Model 85D

Mossberg Model 190D

Mossberg Model 195D

**Mossberg Model 190D**
Same as 185D except 16 gauge
**Estimated Value: $65.00 - $85.00**

**Mossberg Model 195D**
Same as 185D except 12 gauge
**Estimated Value: $75.00 - $95.00**

**Mossberg Model 85D & 185D**
**Gauge:** 20
**Action:** Bolt action; repeating
**Magazine:** 2-shot detachable box
**Barrel:** 25" on 85D, 26" on 185D;
interchangeable choke fittings
**Finish:** Blued; hardwood pistol grip
one-piece stock & forearm; called
185D after 1948
**Estimated Value: $75.00 - $95.00**

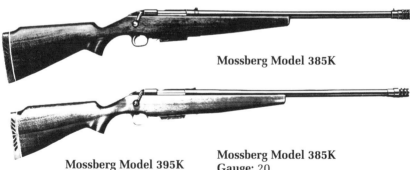

Mossberg Model 385K

Mossberg Model 395K

**Mossberg Model 395K**
Same as 385K in 12 gauge
**Estimated Value: $75.00 - $100.00**

**Mossberg Model 385K**
**Gauge:** 20
**Action:** Bolt action; repeating
**Magazine:** 2-shot detachable box
**Barrel:** 26" adjustable choke
**Finish:** Blued; wood Monte Carlo
semi-pistol grip one-piece stock &
tapered forearm; recoil pad
**Estimated Value: $75.00 - $100.00**

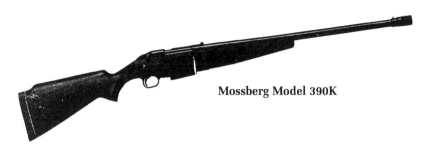

Mossberg Model 390K

**Mossberg Model 585**
Similar to the Model 385K with improved safety
**Estimated Value: $90.00 - $120.00**

**Mossberg Model 390 K**
Similar to the 385K except: 16 gauge; 28" adjustable choke barrel
**Estimated Value: $75.00 - $95.00**

**Mossberg Model 595**
Similar to the Model 395K except: improved safety; 28" adjustable choke barrel
**Estimated Value: $90.00 - $120.00**

**Mossberg Model 395 SPL**
Similar to the Model 395K with a 38" full choke waterfowl barrel; swivels
**Estimated Value: $100.00 - $125.00**

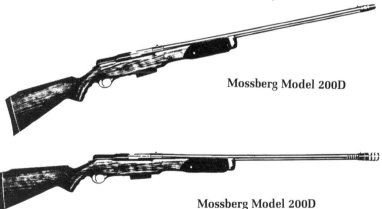

Mossberg Model 200D

Mossberg Model 200K

**Mossberg Model 200K**
Similar to the 200D with adjustable choke
**Estimated Value: $100.00 - $125.00**

**Mossberg Model 200D**
**Gauge:** 12
**Action:** Slide action; hammerless; repeating; slide handle is metal cover over wood forearm
**Magazine:** 3-shot detachable box
**Barrel:** 28" interchangeable choke fittings
**Finish:** Blued; wood Monte Carlo semi-pistol grip one-piece stock & forearm
**Estimated Value: $90.00 - $115.00**

# Mossberg

## Mossberg Model 3000 Field
**Gauge:** 12 or 20; regular or magnum
**Action:** Slide action; hammerless; repeating
**Magazine:** 4-shot tubular, 3-shot in magnum
**Barrel:** 26" improved cylinder, 28" modified or full, 30" full; ventilated rib; "Multi-choke" optional; add 10% for "Multi-choke"
**Finish:** Checkered walnut pistol grip stock & slide handle
**Estimated Value: $200.00 - $265.00**

## Mossberg Model 3000 Waterfowler
Similar to the Model 3000 except: 30" full choke barrel only; parkerized oiled finish or camo finish with "Speedfeed" storage stock; add 10% for "Speedfeed" storage stock or "Multi-choke"
**Estimated Value: $215.00 - $290.00**

## Mossberg Model 3000 Slug
Similar to the Model 3000 except: 22" slug barrel & rifle sights; black finish and "speedfeed storage stock;" add $35.00 for black finish with "Speedfeed" storage stock
**Estimated Value: $185.00 - $250.00**

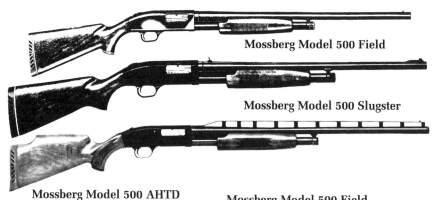

Mossberg Model 500 Field

Mossberg Model 500 Slugster

Mossberg Model 500 AHTD

## Mossberg Model 500 Slugster
Similar to 500 field except: 18" or 24" slug barrel & rifle sights; add 20% for removable chokes; add 15% for Trophy Model; add 12% for rifled barrel
**Estimated Value: $155.00 - $205.00**

## Mossberg Model 500 Hi-Rib Trap, AHTD, AHT
Similar to 500 field except: high rib barrel & Monte Carlo stock; AHTD adjustable choke; AHT full choke; 28" or 30" barrel
**Estimated Value: $200.00 - $270.00**

## Mossberg Model 500 Field
**Gauge:** 12, 16, 20, or 410
**Action:** Slide action; hammerless; repeating
**Magazine:** 5-shot tubular
**Barrel:** 24" in Junior Model; 26" adjustable choke or improved cylinder; 28" modified or full; 30" full choke (12 gauge only); "Accu-Choke" optional; add 3% for "Accu-Choke;" vent rib optional; add 8% for vent rib
**Finish:** Blued; walnut pistol grip stock & grooved slide handle; recoil pad; optional camo finish & "Speedfeed" stock after 1985 (add 25% for camo finish & "Speedfeed" stock)
**Estimated Value: $165.00 - $205.00**

*Pocket Guide to Shotguns*

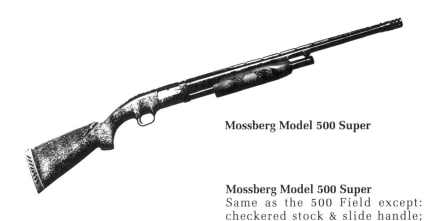

**Mossberg Model 500 Super**

**Mossberg Model 500 Super**
Same as the 500 Field except:
checkered stock & slide handle;
ventilated rib; 12 gauge magnum
**Estimated Value: $175.00 - $215.00**

**Mossberg Model 500 ALDR,
CLDR, ALDRX**
Similar to 500 field in 12 gauge
(ALDR); 20 gauge (CLDR) with
removable choke; (ALDRX) slugster
barrel
**Estimated Value: $160.00 - $200.00**

**Mossberg Model 500 ALMR
Duck Gun**
Same as 500 field except: 12 gauge
magnum; 30" or 32" vent rib barrel
**Estimated Value: $170.00 - $210.00**

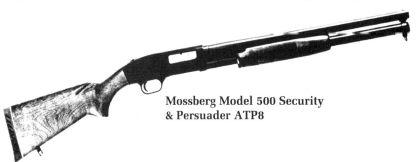

**Mossberg Model 500 Security
& Persuader ATP8**

**Mossberg Model 500 Security &
Persuader ATP6**
Similar to the Model 500 field
except: built in several models for
law enforcement use; 12 gauge, 6-
shot, 18½" barrel; add 17% for
Parkerized finish; add 9% for rifle
sights; add 26% for nickel finish;
add 13% for "Speedfeed" stock; add
22% for camo finish
**Estimated Value: $150.00 - $185.00**

**Mossberg Model 500 Security &
Persuader ATP8**
Similar to the Model 500 ATP6
series except: 20" barrel; 8-shot
capacity; add 8% for rifle sights;
16% for parkerized finish; 24% for
nickel finish; 12% for "Speedfeed"
stock; 20% for camo finish
**Estimated Value: $150.00 - $185.00**

# Mossberg

Mossberg Model 500 ER

## Mossberg Model 500 Persuader Cruiser
Similar to the Model 500 ATP6 and ATP8 series law enforcement shotguns except: one-hand grip; add 26% for nickel finish
Estimated Value: $145.00 - $180.00

## Mossberg Model 500 Mariner
Similar to the Persuader series except: special Teflon & metal coating that is resistant to salt water spray; stock & slide handle are synthetic;  6 or 9-shot; add 20% for 9-shot model; 10% for "Speedfeed" stock
Estimated Value: $200.00 - $250.00

## Mossberg Model 500 APR Pigeon
Similar to the 500 Field except: engraving; ventilated rib
Estimated Value: $190.00 - $260.00

## Mossberg Model 500 ARTP Trap
Similar to the 500 APR except: 30" full choke barrel; Monte Carlo stock
Estimated Value: $200.00 - $275.00

## Mossberg Model 500 Camper
Similar to the Model 500 Persuader Cruiser in 12 gauge, 20 gauge, or 410 bore; 18½" barrel; synthetic grip & slide handle; camo carrying case
Estimated Value: $170.00 - $210.00

## Mossberg Model 500 ER, ELR
Similar to the 500 Field except: 410 gauge; 26" barrel; skeet version; checkering & ventilated rib
Estimated Value: $150.00 - $200.00

## Mossberg 500 Security & Persuader CTP6, ETP6
Similar to the other 500 series law enforcement shotguns in 20 gauge (CTP6) or 410 bore (ETP6); 18½" barrel; 6-shot
Estimated Value: $150.00 - $190.00

## Mossberg Model 500 Regal
Similar to the Model 500 field except: deluxe finish; crown design on receiver; add $20.00 for "Accu-Choke"
Estimated Value: $165.00 - $210.00

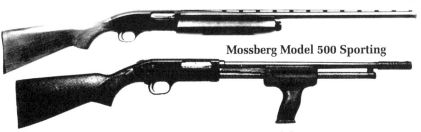

### Mossberg Model 500 Sporting

### Mossberg Model HS 410 Home Security

### Mossberg Model 500 Sporting
**Gauge:** 12, 20, or 410; regular or magnum
**Action:** Slide action, hammerless; repeating; double slide bars
**Magazine:** 5-shot tubular
**Barrel:** 20", 24", 26", or 28"; "Accu-Choke" tubes or fixed choke; plain or ventilated rib
**Finish:** Blued or camo; add 8% for camo finish; checkered walnut finish stock and slide handle or synthetic stock and slide handle; add 18% for ghost ring sights
**Estimated Value: $165.00 - $205.00**

### Mossberg Model HS 410 Home Security
**Gauge:** 410; 3" chamber
**Action:** Slide action, hammerless; repeating
**Magazine:** 4-shot tubular
**Barrel:** 18½" with muzzle brake and spreader choke (the spreader choke delivers almost twice the size circle of a regular shotgun pattern)
**Finish:** Blued with synthetic stock and slide handle; the laser light sight model has a vertical hand grip slide which contain the light and battery; add 82% for laser light model
**Estimated Value: $185.00 - $230.00**

### Mossberg 835 Camo Ulti-Mag

### Mossberg 835 Field Grade Ulti-Mag
**Gauge:** 12 (3½" chamber); regular or magnum
**Action:** Slide action, hammerless; repeating; double slide bars
**Magazine:** 4 or 5-shot tubular
**Barrel:** 24" or 28"; with ventilated rib; "Accu-Mag" Choke tube or 24" with rifle sights and cylinder bore fixed choke; deduct 4% for 24" fixed cylinder bore choke barrel with rifle sights
**Finish:** Blued, walnut-finish, checkered stock and slide handle
**Estimated Value: $170.00 - $210.00**

### Mossberg 835 Regal Ulti-Mag
Same as 835 Field Grade Ulti-Mag except: walnut stock and slide handle; dual-comb stock (stock comb height can be changed by removing one bolt); 24" rifle bore barrel with scope base optional; add 5% for 24" rifle bore barrel
**Estimated Value: $225.00 - $280.00**

### Mossberg 835 Camo Ulti-Mag
Same as 835 Regal Ulti-Mag except: camo finish; the National Wild Turkey Federation (NWTF) Model has synthetic stock (without dual comb feature) and slide handle with "Realtree" Camo pattern and 24" barrel with x-full tube Accu-Mag choke; add 7% for the NWTF Model
**Estimated Value: $240.00 - $300.00**

# Mossberg

Mossberg Model 5500

Mossberg Model 5500 Slugster

Mossberg Model 9200

## Mossberg Model 9200
**Gauge:** 12, regular or magnum
**Action:** Gas operated semi-automatic; a gas regulating system compensates for varied pressures from normal to magnum loads
**Magazine:** 4-shot; 3-shot in magnum
**Barrel:** 24" rifled bore; 24" or 28" smooth bore with Accu-Choke tubes; wide ventilated rib, white front bead and brass midpoint bead
**Finish:** Blued or camo; checkered pistol grip walnut finish stock and forearm; camo finish has synthetic stock and forearm; add 65% for camo finish; the 24" rifled bore has walnut finish dual-comb stock in blued finish; add 6% for 24" rifled bore with dual comb stock
**Estimated Value: $225.00 - $280.00**

## Mossberg Model 5500
**Gauge:** 12, regular or magnum
**Action:** Gas operated semi-automatic
**Magazine:** 4-shot tubular
**Barrel:** 25" (youth model); 26" improved cylinder, 28" modified, 30" full, or 28" "Accu-Choke" with interchangeable tubes; ventilated rib optional
**Finish:** Blued; checkered hardwood or synthetic semi-pistol grip stock & forearm; aluminum alloy receiver; youth model has smaller stock
**Estimated Value: $225.00 - $280.00**

## Mossberg Model 5500 Slugster
Similar to the Model 5500 except: 18½" or 24" slug barrel; rifle sights & swivels
**Estimated Value: $255.00 - $335.00**

Mossberg Model 1000 Field

**Mossberg Model 1000 Super Skeet**
Similar to the Model 1000 Super with 25" skeet barrel
**Estimated Value: $370.00 - $495.00**

**Mossberg Model 1000 Super**
**Gauge:** 12 or 20, regular or magnum
**Action:** Gas operated semi-automatic
**Magazine:** 3-shot tubular
**Barrel:** 26", 28", or 30" "Multi-choke;" ventilated rib
**Finish:** Blued; checkered walnut pistol grip stock & forearm; recoil pad; scrolling on receiver
**Estimated Value: $300.00 - $400.00**

**Mossberg Model 1000 Field**
Similar to the Model 1000 Super except: alloy receiver; various chokes available including a 26" skeet barrel; add $30.00 for "Multi-choke;" Junior model has 22" barrel with "Multi-choke;" add 15% for Junior model
**Estimated Value: $245.00 - $330.00**

**Mossberg Model 1000 Super Waterfowler**
Similar to the Model 1000 Super except: dull wood & Parkerized finish; 12 gauge only
**Estimated Value: $315.00 - $420.00**

**Mossberg Model 1000 Slug**
Similar to the Model 1000 Field except: 22" slug barrel with rifle sights
**Estimated Value: $240.00 - $320.00**

**Mossberg Model 1000 Trap**
Similar to the Model 1000 Field except: 30" "Multi-choke" barrel, recoil pad, Monte Carlo stock & high-rib barrel
**Estimated Value: $315.00 - $420.00**

**Mossberg Model 1000 Super Slug**
Similar to the Model 1000 Super with 22" slug barrel
**Estimated Value: $295.00 - $395.00**

**Mossberg 712 Camo**

**Mossberg Model 712 Camo**
Similar to the Model 712 except: camo finish & "Speedfeed" storage stock; add 15% for "Accu-Choke"
Estimated Value: $220.00 - $290.00

**Mossberg Model 712 Regal**
Same as Model 712 except: deluxe finish, crown design on receiver; add 15% for "Accu-Choke"
Estimated Value: $200.00 - $275.00

**Mossberg Model 712**
Gauge: 12, regular or magnum
Action: Gas operated semi-automatic; designed to handle any 12 gauge shell interchangeably
Magazine: 4-shot tubular, 3-shot in magnum
Barrel: 30" full, 28" modified, 24" "Accu-choke;" add 15% for "Accu-choke;" 24" slug model; add 8% for slug model with rifle sights; ventilated rib optional; add 8% for ventilated rib
Finish: Alloy receiver with anodized finish; checkered walnut finish semi-pistol grip stock & forearm; recoil pad; Junior Model has 13" stock.
Estimated Value: $205.00 - $260.00

# New England

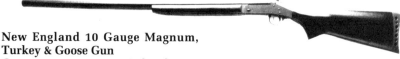

**New England 10 Gauge Magnum, Turkey & Goose Gun**
Gauge: 10 magnum; 3½" chamber
Action: Side lever release, break-open; single shot; exposed hammer
Magazine: None, single shot
Barrel: 28" or 32" full choke
Finish: Blued; hardwood walnut finish, smooth, pistol grip stock & forearm; recoil pad; also camo matte finish stock & forearm (after 1991); add 12% for camo finish
Estimated Value: $105.00 - $130.00

**New England 10 Gauge Magnum**

**New England Turkey**
Similar to the 10 gauge magnum turkey & goose gun except: 24" barrel; "Mossy oak" or "Bottom land" camo finish
Estimated Value: $80.00 - $100.00

## New England Pardner

### New England Deluxe Pardner
Same as the Pardner except: 12 or 20 gauge only; special double back-up butt stock (holds two spare shells) & recoil pad
**Estimated Value: $95.00 - $120.00**

### New England Pardner
**Gauge:** 12, 16, 20, 28, or 410; also 12 magnum
**Action:** side lever release; break-open; single shot; exposed hammer
**Magazine:** None, single shot
**Barrel:** 24", 26", or 28"; full, modified, or cylinder bore
**Finish:** Blued with color case hardened receiver; hardwood walnut finish pistol grip, smooth stock & lipped forearm
**Estimated Value: $75.00 - $95.00**

### New England Mini-Pardner
Same as the Pardner except: 20 or 410 gauge only, 18½" barrel; short stock; equipped with swivel studs
**Estimated Value: $90.00 - $110.00**

### New England Protector
**Gauge:** 12
**Action:** side lever release, break-open; single shot; exposed hammer
**Magazine:** None, single shot
**Barrel:** 18½" plain
**Finish:** Blued or nickel; add 8% for nickel finish; smooth hardwood walnut finish pistol grip stock & lipped forearm; recoil pad; special double back-up butt stock holds two spare shells; swivels
**Estimated Value: $100.00 - $125.00**

### New England Youth Pardner
Same as the Pardner except: 20 or 410 gauge only with 22" barrel & straight grip, shorter stock with recoil pad
**Estimated Value: $80.00 - $100.00**

# New Haven

## New Haven Model 273

### New Haven Model 273
**Gauge:** 20
**Action:** Bolt action; hammerless; single shot
**Magazine:** None
**Barrel:** 24" full choke
**Finish:** Blued; plain walnut Monte Carlo semi-pistol grip one-piece stock & forearm
**Estimated Value: $60.00 - $75.00**

# New Haven

New Haven Model 290

**New Haven Model 290**
**Gauge:** 16
**Action:** Bolt action; hammerless; repeating
**Magazine:** 2-shot detachable box
**Barrel:** 28"; removable full choke
**Finish:** Blued; walnut Monte Carlo pistol grip one-piece stock & tapered forearm
**Estimated Value: $65.00 - $85.00**

**New Haven Model 283 or 283T**
A 410 gauge version of the 290 with a 24" barrel; also called 283T
**Estimated Value: $70.00 - $90.00**

**New Haven Model 295**
A 12 gauge version of the 290
**Estimated Value: $60.00 - $80.00**

**New Haven Model 285**
A 20 gauge version of the model 290 with 24" barrel
**Estimated Value: $65.00 - $85.00**

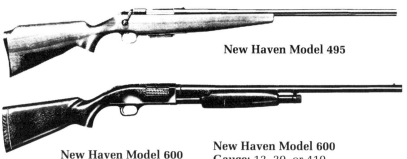

New Haven Model 495

New Haven Model 600

**New Haven Model 495, 495T**
**Gauge:** 12
**Action:** Bolt action; hammerless; repeating
**Magazine:** 2-shot detachable box
**Barrel:** 28" full choke
**Finish:** Blued; walnut Monte Carlo semi-pistol grip stock & tapered forearm
**Estimated Value: $85.00 - $110.00**

**New Haven Model 485T**
A 20 gauge version of the Model 495 with 26" barrel
**Estimated Value: $90.00 - $120.00**

**New Haven Model 600**
**Gauge:** 12, 20, or 410
**Action:** Slide action; hammerless; repeating
**Magazine:** 6-shot tubular
**Barrel:** 26" improved cylinder, 28" modified or full, 30" full choke; ventilated rib optional; add 20% for ventilated rib; adjustable choke; add 10% for adjustable choke; changeable choke tubes; add 6% for changeable choke tubes
**Finish:** Blued; walnut semi-pistol grip stock & slide handle
**Estimated Value: $140.00 - $175.00**

**New Haven Model 600 AST**
Similar to Model 600 with 24" barrel & rifle sights
**Estimated Value: $145.00 - $180.00**

# Noble

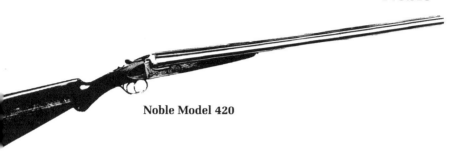

Noble Model 420

**Noble Model 420**
**Gauge:** 12, 16, or 20
**Action:** Box lock; top lever, break-open; hammerless; double triggers
**Magazine:** None
**Barrel:** Double barrel (side by side); 28" modified & full choke
**Finish:** Blued; checkered walnut pistol grip stock & forearm
**Estimated Value: $200.00 - $250.00**

**Noble Model 420 EK**
A fancy version of the Model 420 with automatic ejectors; select walnut; recoil pad; engraving; gold inlay
**Estimated Value: $240.00 - $300.00**

**Noble Model 450E**
Similar to Model 420 EK; made from the late 1960's to the early 1970's
**Estimated Value: $275.00 - $350.00**

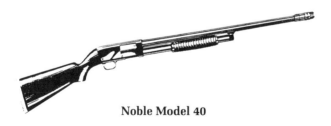

Noble Model 40

**Noble Model 50**
Same as the Model 40 without recoil pad or "Multi-Choke"
**Estimated Value: $105.00 - $130.00**

**Noble Model 40**
**Gauge:** 12
**Action:** Slide action; hammerless
**Magazine:** 5-shot tubular
**Barrel:** 28" with multi-choke
**Finish:** Blued; plain walnut pistol grip stock & grooved slide handle; recoil pad
**Estimated Value: $120.00 - $150.00**

# Noble

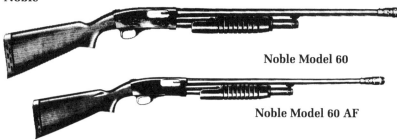

Noble Model 60

Noble Model 60 AF

**Noble Model 60**
**Gauge:** 12 or 16
**Action:** Slide action; hammerless
**Magazine:** 5-shot tubular
**Barrel:** 28" with variable choke
**Finish:** Blued; plain walnut pistol
grip stock & grooved slide handle;
recoil pad
**Estimated Value: $115.00 - $145.00**

**Noble Model 60 AF**
A fancier version of the Model 60
with special steel barrel; select
wood; fluted comb stock
**Estimated Value: $125.00 - $160.00**

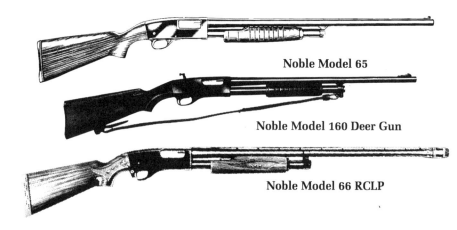

Noble Model 65

Noble Model 160 Deer Gun

Noble Model 66 RCLP

**Noble Model 65**
Same as the Model 60 except:
without the recoil pad; without
variable choke
**Estimated Value: $100.00 - $130.00**

**Noble Model 160 Deer Gun, 166L
Deer Gun**
Similar to the Model 60 except: 24"
barrel; sights; swivels; made in the
mid 1960's as model 160; from late
1960's to early 1970's as model 166L
**Estimated Value: $130.00 - $165.00**

**Noble Model 60 ACP**
Same as the Model 60 except: it has
ventilated rib
**Estimated Value: $125.00 - $160.00**

**Noble Model 66 RCLP**
Similar to the Model 60 ACP with a
fancier checkered stock
**Estimated Value: $125.00 - $160.00**

Noble Model 70

Noble Model 602

Noble Model 602 CLP

## Noble Model 602, CLP, RCLP, RLP
Similar to the Model 70 except: 20 gauge; 28" barrel; grooved slide handle; CLP has adjustable choke; RCLP has recoil pad; RLP has recoil pad & ventilated rib; add 10% for ventilated rib
**Estimated Value: $145.00 - $180.00**

## Noble Model 70 & 70X
**Gauge:** 410
**Action:** Slide action; hammerless
**Magazine:** 5-shot tubular
**Barrel:** 26" modified or full choke
**Finish:** Blued; checkered walnut pistol grip stock & slide handle; made from the late 1950's to late 1960's as Model 70; late 1960's to early 1970's as 70X
**Estimated Value: $130.00 - $165.00**

Noble Model 246

## Noble Model 249
**Gauge:** 20
**Action:** Slide action; hammerless
**Magazine:** 5-shot tubular
**Barrel:** 28" modified or full choke
**Finish:** Blued; checkered walnut pistol grip stock & slide handle; recoil pad
**Estimated Value: $125.00 - $160.00**

## Noble Model 246
Same as Model 249 except: adjustable choke
**Estimated Value: $135.00 - $170.00**

## Noble Model 243
Same as Model 249 except: it has ventilated rib
**Estimated Value: $140.00 - $175.00**

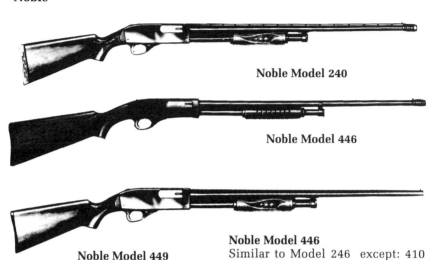

Noble Model 240

Noble Model 446

Noble Model 449

**Noble Model 446**
Similar to Model 246 except: 410 bore; no recoil pad
**Estimated Value: $125.00 - $165.00**

**Noble Model 240**
Same as Model 249 except: it has adjustable choke & ventilated rib
**Estimated Value: $145.00 - $185.00**

**Noble Model 443**
Similar to Model 243 except: 410 bore; no recoil pad
**Estimated Value: $130.00 - $170.00**

**Noble Model 449**
Same as the Model 249 except: 410 bore; no recoil pad
**Estimated Value: $125.00 - $165.00**

**Noble Model 440**
Similar to Model 240 except: 410 bore; no recoil pad
**Estimated Value: $135.00 - $180.00**

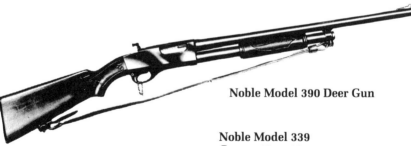

Noble Model 390 Deer Gun

**Noble Model 390 Deer Gun**
Similar to Model 339 except: 24" slug barrel; sights; swivels
**Estimated Value: $140.00 - $175.00**

**Noble Model 339**
**Gauge:** 12 or 16
**Action:** Slide action; hammerless
**Magazine:** 6-shot tubular
**Barrel:** 28" modified or full choke
**Finish:** Blued; checkered walnut pistol grip stock & slide handle
**Estimated Value: $130.00 - $165.00**

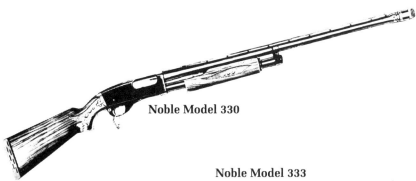

Noble Model 330

**Noble Model 333**
Same as Model 339 except: it has
recoil pad & ventilated rib
**Estimated Value: $135.00 - $180.00**

**Noble Model 330**
Same as Model 339 with recoil pad,
ventilated rib, & adjustable choke
**Estimated Value: $185.00 - $140.00**

**Noble Model 336**
Same as Model 339 except: it has
recoil pad & adjustable choke
**Estimated Value: $140.00 - $175.00**

Noble Model 80

**Noble Model 80**
**Gauge:** 410
**Action:** Semi-automatic; hammerless
**Magazine:** 5-shot tubular
**Barrel:** 26" full choke
**Finish:** Blued; plain walnut pistol
grip stock & forearm
**Estimated Value: $175.00 - $220.00**

**Noble Model 757**
**Gauge:** 20
**Action:** Slide action; hammerless
**Magazine:** 5-shot tubular
**Barrel:** 28" aluminum; adjustable
choke
**Finish:** Black anodized aluminum;
decorated receiver; checkered
walnut pistol grip stock & slide
handle; recoil pad
**Estimated Value: $130.00 - $175.00**

# Parker

## Parker Trojan
**Gauge:** 12, 16, or 20
**Action:** Top lever break-open; hammerless; box lock
**Magazine:** None
**Barrel:** Double barrel (side by side); 26", 28", or 30", full & full or modified & full chokes
**Finish:** Blued; checkered walnut pistol grip stock & forearm
**Estimated Value:** $1,000.00 - $1,500.00

Parker Single Barrel Trap

Parker Trojan

## Parker Hammerless Double
**Gauge:** 10, 12, 16, 20, 28, or 410
**Action:** Box lock; top lever, break-open; hammerless; selective trigger & automatic ejectors after 1934
**Magazine:** None
**Barrel:** Double barrel (side by side); 26", 28", 30", or 32"; any choke combination
**Finish:** Blued; checkered walnut straight, full or semi-pistol grip stock & forearm; grades vary according to workmanship, checkering & engraving; manufacture of Parker guns was taken over by Remington in 1934; Priced for pre-1934 models
**Estimated Value:**
$1,200.00 - $50,000.00

## Parker Single Barrel Trap
**Gauge:** 12
**Action:** Slide action; hammerless; top lever break-open; box lock; single shot
**Magazine:** None; single shot
**Barrel:** 30", 32", or 34", any choke; ventilated rib
**Finish:** Blued; checkered walnut straight, full or semi-pistol grip stock; grades differ according to workmanship, checkering, & engraving; manufacture of Parker guns was taken over by Remington in 1934, & this gun was called Remington Parker Model 930; there is a wide range of values for this gun.
**Estimated Value:**
$2,000.00 - $12,000.00

**Pedersen Model 2500**

## Pedersen Model 2000 Grade II
**Gauge:** 12 or 20
**Action:** Box lock; top lever, break-open; hammerless; automatic ejectors; single selective trigger
**Magazine:** None
**Barrel:** Double barrel (side by side); length to customer's specifications
**Finish:** Blued; checkered walnut pistol grip stock & tapered forearm; engraved
**Estimated Value: $1,200.00 - $1,500.00**

## Pedersen Model 2000 Grade I
Similar to Grade II with fancier engraving, gold filling on receiver, select walnut
**Estimated Value: $1,450.00 - $1,800.00**

## Pedersen Model 2500
A field grade version of the model 2000; no engraving; blade front
**Estimated Value: $350.00 - $450.00**

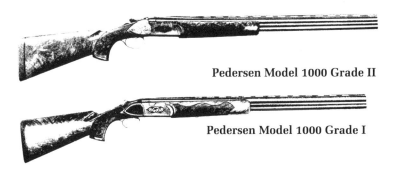

**Pedersen Model 1000 Grade II**

**Pedersen Model 1000 Grade I**

## Pedersen Model 1000 Grade III
**Gauge:** 12 or 20
**Action:** Box lock; top lever, break-open; hammerless; automatic ejectors; single selective trigger
**Magazine:** None
**Barrel:** Over & under double barrel; length made to customers specifications; ventilated rib
**Finish:** Blued; checkered walnut pistol grip stock & forearm; recoil pad
**Estimated Value: $600.00 - $800.00**

## Pedersen Model 1000 Grade II
Similar to Model 1000 Grade III except: engraving & fancier wood; made to customers specs.
**Estimated Value: $1,400.00 - $1,725.00**

## Pedersen Model 1000 Grade I
Similar to Model 1000 Grade II except: extensive engraving, select wood, gold filling on receiver; made to customers specs;  hunting, skeet, or trap models
**Estimated Value: $1,750.00 - $2,100.00**

## Pedersen/Premier

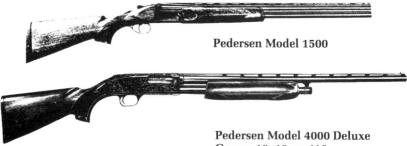

Pedersen Model 1500

Pedersen Model 4000 Deluxe

**Pedersen Model 4000 Deluxe**
**Gauge:** 10, 12, or 410
**Action:** Slide action; hammerless;
side ejection
**Magazine:** 5-shot Tubular
**Barrel:** 26", 28", or 30", variety of
chokes; ventilated rib
**Finish:** Blued; checkered walnut
pistol grip stock & slide handle;
recoil pad; floral engraving on
receiver
**Estimated Value: $320.00 - $400.00**

**Pedersen Model 1500**
A field version of the Model 1000
Grade III except: standard barrel
lengths (26", 28", 30, or 32")
**Estimated Value: $400.00 - $500.00**

# Premier

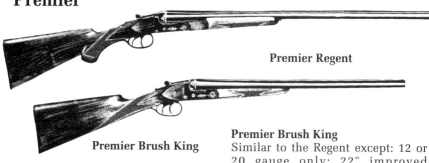

Premier Regent

Premier Brush King

**Premier Brush King**
Similar to the Regent except: 12 or
20 gauge only; 22" improved
cylinder & modified choke barrels;
straight stock
**Estimated Value: $225.00 - $285.00**

**Premier Regent**
**Gauge:** 12, 16, 20, 28, or 410
**Action:** Box lock; top lever, break-
open; hammerless; double triggers
**Magazine:** None
**Barrel:** Double barrel (side by side);
26" or 28" modified & full choke;
matte rib
**Finish:** Blued; checkered walnut
pistol grip stock & tapered forearm
**Estimated Value: $220.00 - $275.00**

**Premier Magnum**
Similar to the Regent except: 10
gauge magnum with 32" barrels or 12
gauge magnum with 30" barrels; both
gauges in full & full choke; recoil
pad; beavertail forearm; add 10% for
20 gauge magnum
**Estimated Value: $240.00 - $300.00**

Premier Continental

**Premier Ambassador**
A hammerless version of the Continental. Also available in 410 gauge.
**Estimated Value: $350.00 - $280.00**

**Premier Continental**
**Gauge:** 12, 16, or 20
**Action:** Side lock; top lever, break-open; exposed hammers; double triggers
**Magazine:** None
**Barrel:** Double barrel (side by side); 26" modified & full choke
**Finish:** Blued; checkered walnut pistol grip stock & tapered forearm
**Estimated Value: $260.00 - $325.00**

Premier Ambassador

# Remington

**Remington Model 1893**
**Gauge:** 10, 12, 16, or 20
**Action:** Top lever, break-open; semi-hammer (cocking lever on left), takedown; single shot
**Magazine:** None; single shot
**Barrel:** 28", 30", 32", or 34"; plain barrel
**Finish:** Blued; case hardened receiver; smooth walnut, pistol grip stock & forearm; also known as the Model No. 3 & the '93
**Estimated Value: $155.00 - $195.00**

**Remington Model 1902 or No. 9**
Similar to the Model 1893 except: improved with automatic ejector; made from about 1902 to 1912; also called Model No. 9
**Estimated Value: $165.00 - $200.00**

**Remington Parker 930**
Remington took over production of the Parker shotguns from 1934 to 1941; single shot hammerless
**Estimated Value: $1,000.00 - $2,500.00**

# Remington

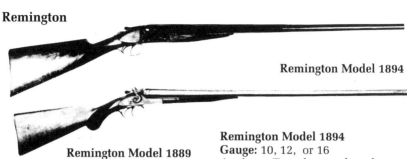

Remington Model 1894

Remington Model 1889

## Remington Model 1894
**Gauge:** 10, 12, or 16
**Action:** Top lever, break-open; concealed hammers; triple lock; double triggers; some models have automatic ejectors
**Magazine:** None
**Barrel:** Double barrel (side by side); 26"-32" tapered barrels; full, modified or cylinder bores; ordnance steel or Damascus barrels with concave matted rib
**Finish:** Blued; checkered walnut, straight or semi-pistol grip stock & short tapered forearm; receivers marked Remington Arms Co. on left side; special engraving & inlays on higher grades; made in seven grades; priced for Standard Grade; deduct $150.00 for Damascus barrels
**Estimated Value: $525.00 - $700.00**

## Remington Model 1889
**Gauge:** 10, 12, or 16
**Action:** Top lever, break-open; side lock; breech loading black powder; exposed hammers; double trigger
**Magazine:** None
**Barrel:** Double barrel (side by side); 28"-32" full, modified or cylinder bores; Damascus or steel barrels
**Finish:** Blued; checkered walnut semi-pistol grip stock & short forearm; made in seven grades; priced for Standard Grade
**Estimated Value: $440.00 - $550.00**

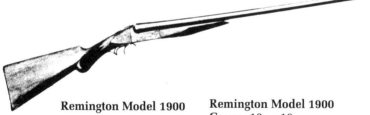

Remington Model 1900

## Remington Model 1900
**Gauge:** 12 or 16
**Action:** Top lever, break-open; concealed hammers; double triggers; automatic ejectors optional
**Magazine:** None
**Barrel:** Double barrel (side by side); 28" or 32" steel or Damascus barrels in standard chokes; deduct $100.00 for Damascus barrels; matted rib
**Finish:** Checkered walnut pistol grip stock & short tapered forearm
**Estimated Value: $400.00 - $500.00**

## Remington Parker 920
Remington took over production of Parker shotguns from 1934 to 1941; double barrel hammerless; double triggers; 12 gauge
**Estimated Value: $750.00 - $1,000.00**

*Pocket Guide to Shotguns*

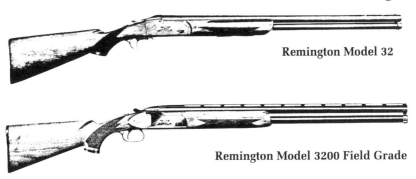

Remington Model 32

Remington Model 3200 Field Grade

## Remington Model 32
**Gauge:** 12
**Action:** Top lever, break-open; concealed hammers; single selective trigger; automatic ejectors
**Magazine:** None
**Barrel:** Over & under double barrel; 26-32" plain; solid or ventilated rib; add 5% for solid rib; add 10% for ventilated rib; full & modified choke standard but any combination available
**Finish:** Blued; engraved receiver; checkered walnut pistol grip stock & forearm; made in about six grades; priced for standard grade
**Estimated Value: $600.00 - $750.00**

## Remington Model 3200 Field Grade
**Gauge:** 12
**Action:** Top lever, break-open; concealed hammers; selective single trigger; automatic ejectors
**Magazine:** None
**Barrel:** 26"-30" over & under double barrel; ventilated rib; modified & full or improved cylinder & modified chokes
**Finish:** Blued; pointing dogs engraved on receiver; checkered walnut pistol grip stock & matching forearm; priced for field grade
**Estimated Value: $700.00 - $875.00**

Remington Model 3200 Magnum

## Remington Model 3200 Special Trap
Similar to the Model 3200 except: 32" barrels; ventilated rib; Monte Carlo stock; recoil pad
**Estimated Value: $950.00 - $1,200.00**

## Remington Model 3200 Magnum
Similar to the Model 3200 Field Grade except: chambered for 12 gauge magnum; 30" barrels in full & full or modified & full chokes; receiver decorated with engraved scrollwork
**Estimated Value: $790.00 - $990.00**

# Remington

Remington Model 3200 Skeet

**Remington Model 3200 Competition Trap**
Similar to the Model 3200 Special Trap except: higher quality finish
Estimated Value: $975.00 - $1,300.00

**Remington Model 3200 Competition Skeet**
Similar to the Model 3200 Skeet except: higher quality finish
Estimated Value: $975.00 - $1,300.00

**Remington Model 3200 Skeet**
Similar to the Model 3200 except: 26" or 28" skeet barrels; ventilated rib ; recoil pad; Monte Carlo stock
Estimated Value: $825.00 - $1,100.00

**Remington Model 3200 Pigeon**
Similar to the Model 3200 Competition Skeet except: 28" improved modified & full choke barrels for bird hunting
Estimated Value: $1,000.00 - $1,325.00

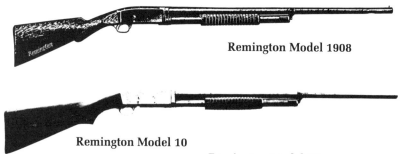

Remington Model 1908

Remington Model 10

**Remington Model 1908**
**Gauge:** 12
**Action:** Slide action; hammerless; bottom ejection; repeating
**Magazine:** 5-shot tubular
**Barrel:** 26"-32" steel barrel in full, modified or cylinder bore
**Finish:** Blued; plain or checkered walnut straight or pistol grip stock & forearm; made in six grades with fancy checkering & engraving on higher grades; priced for field grade
Estimated Value: $250.00 - $325.00

**Remington Model 10**
**Gauge:** 12
**Action:** Slide action; hammerless; bottom ejection; repeating
**Magazine:** 5-shot tubular
**Barrel:** 20" barrel riot gun; 26"-32" steel barrel in full, modified or cylinder bore; plain barrel; ventilated or solid rib optional
**Finish:** Blued; plain or checkered walnut straight or pistol grip stock & forearm; an improved version of the Model 1908; made in seven grades; priced for field grade
Estimated Value: $275.00 - $350.00

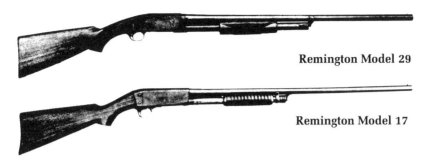

**Remington Model 29**

**Remington Model 17**

**Remington Model 29**
**Gauge:** 12
**Action:** Slide action; hammerless; bottom ejection; repeating
**Magazine:** 5-shot tubular
**Barrel:** 26"-32" steel in full, modified or cylinder bore; optional solid or ventilated rib; 20" barrel on riot gun
**Finish:** Blued; plain or checkered walnut pistol grip stock & forearm; made in nine grades; priced for field grade
**Estimated Value:** $215.00 - $280.00

**Remington Model 17**
**Gauge:** 20
**Action:** Slide action; hammerless; bottom ejection; repeating
**Magazine:** 3-shot tubular
**Barrel:** 26"-32" steel in full, modified or cylinder bore; matted sighting groove on receiver or optional solid rib; 20" barrel on riot gun
**Finish:** Blued; plain or checkered walnut pistol grip stock & forearm; made in seven grades; priced for field grade
**Estimated Value:** $205.00 - $275.00

**Remington Model 31**

**Remington Model 31 Skeet**
Similar to the Model 31 except: 12 gauge only; 26" barrel; solid or ventilated rib; skeet choke; add 8% for ventilated rib
**Estimated Value:** $360.00 - $450.00

**Remington Model 31 R Riot Gun**
Similar to the Model 31 except: 12 gauge only; 20" plain barrel
**Estimated Value:** $170.00 - $225.00

**Remington Model 31**
**Gauge:** 12, 16, or 20
**Action:** Slide action; hammerless; side ejection; repeating
**Magazine:** 3-shot tubular or 5-shot tubular
**Barrel:** 26", 32" steel; full, modified, cylinder, or skeet chokes; solid or ventilated rib optional
**Finish:** Blued; plain or checkered pistol grip stock & forearm; forearm checkered or grooved; made in eight grades; priced for field grade; add 10% for solid rib or ventilated rib
**Estimated Value:** $220.00 - $275.00

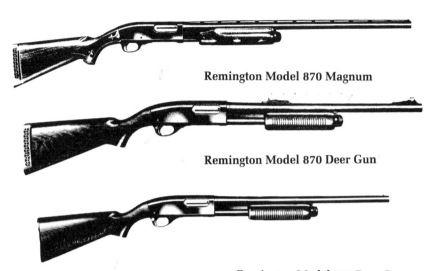

Remington Model 870 Magnum

Remington Model 870 Deer Gun

Remington Model 870 Riot Gun

## Remington Model 870 Deer Gun
Similar to the Model 870 AP except:
12 gauge only; 26" barrel for slugs;
rifle type adjustable sights
**Estimated Value: $200.00 - $250.00**

## Remington Model 870 AP
**Gauge:** 12, 16, or 20
**Action:** Slide action; hammerless;
side ejection; repeating
**Magazine:** 4-shot tubular
**Barrel:** 26" or 28" in 16 & 20 gauge;
30" in 12 gauge; full, modified or
improved cylinder bore; plain or
ventilated rib; add 10% for ventilated rib
**Finish:** Blued; plain or fancy, fluted
comb, pistol grip stock & grooved
slide handle; made in many grades &
variations; priced for field grade
**Estimated Value: $185.00 - $250.00**

## Remington Model 870 Magnum
Similar to the Model 870 AP except:
12 gauge magnum; 30" full choke
barrel; recoil pad; add 10% for
ventilated rib
**Estimated Value: $195.00 - $260.00**

## Remington Model 870 Riot Gun
Same as the Model 870 AP except:
12 gauge only; 20" plain barrel;
improved cylinder bore
**Estimated Value: $180.00 - $225.00**

## Remington Model 870 Special Purpose
Similar to the Model 870 AP except:
oil-finish wood & Parkerized metal;
recoil pad & nylon camo strap; 12
gauge; ventilated rib, 26" or 30"
barrel; "Rem Choke;" deduct 20%
for synthetic stock
**Estimated Value: $270.00 - $340.00**

## Remington Model 870 SP Deer Gun
Similar to the 870 Special Purpose
except: 20" improved cylinder bore
barrel & rifle sights
**Estimated Value: $265.00 - $330.00**

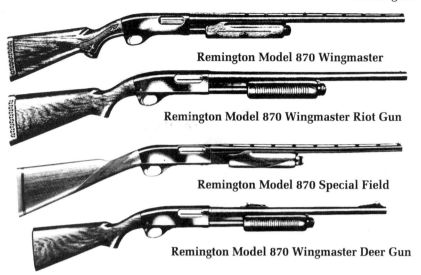

Remington Model 870 Wingmaster

Remington Model 870 Wingmaster Riot Gun

Remington Model 870 Special Field

Remington Model 870 Wingmaster Deer Gun

**Remington Model 870
Wingmaster Field Gun**
Gauge: 12, 16, or 20; 28 & 410 added
in 1969; 16 gauge discontinued in
the late 1980's
Action: Slide action; hammerless;
side ejection; repeating
Magazine: 4-shot tubular
Barrel: 26"-30" in 12 gauge; 26" or
28" in 16 & 20 gauge; 25" in 28 & 410
bore; add 8% for gauges 28 or 410;
full, modified, or improved cylinder
bore; plain or ventilated rib barrel
Finish: Blued; checkered walnut
pistol grip stock with matching slide
handle; recoil pad; lightweight and
left hand models optional; add 10%
for left hand model; made in many
grades; priced for field grade
Estimated Value:   $275.00 - $345.00

**Remington Model 870 Special Field**
Similar   to   the   Model   870
wingmaster except:  straight grip
stock; 21" ventilated rib barrel; 12 or
20  gauge;  3"  chamber;  "Rem
Choke"optional
Estimated Value: $270.00 - $340.00

**Remington Model 870
Wingmaster Magnum**
Same as the Model 870 Field Grade
except: 12 or 20 gauge magnum
only; full or modified choke; add
10% for left hand model; add 10%
for "Rem Choke"
Estimated Value: $260.00 - $325.00

**Remington Model 870 Wingmaster
Riot Gun, Police**
Similar   to   the   Model   870
Wingmaster except: 12 gauge only;
18" or 20" improved cylinder barrel;
plain stock & grooved slide handle;
designed for law enforcement use;
add 8% for rifle sights; blued or
parkerized finish
Estimated Value: $205.00 - $260.00

**Remington Model 870
Wingmaster Deer Gun**
Same as Model 870 Wingmaster
except: 12 gauge only; 20" barrel;
rifle sights
Estimated Value: $255.00 - $315.00

Remington Model 870 Brushmaster Deer Gun

**Remington Model 870 Ltd. 20**
Same as the Model 870 Wingmaster Field except: 20 gauge only; 23" barrel with ventilated rib; lightweight; made from 1980 to 1984
Estimated Value: $310.00 - $250.00

**Remington Model 870 Brushmaster Deer Gun**
Same as the Model 870 Wingmaster Deer Gun except: 12 & 20 gauge; checkered stock & slide; recoil pad; add 8% for 12 gauge
Estimated Value: $250.00 - $310.00

**Remington Model 870SA Skeet**
Similar to the Model 870 wingmaster except: skeet choke; recoil pad; 25" or 26" ventilated rib barrel
Estimated Value: $240.00 - $300.00

**Remington Model 870 TB Trap, TA Trap, TC Trap**
Similar to the Model 870 wingmaster except: 30" full choke ventilated rib barrel; recoil pad
Estimated Value: $320.00 - $400.00

**Remington Model 870 Competition Trap**
Similar in appearance to the Model 870 except: single shot; 30" full choke ventilated rib barrel; recoil pad; non-glare matte finish receiver
Estimated Value: $425.00 - $570.00

**Remington Model 870SP Cantilever**
Same as the Model 870SP Deer Gun except: no sights; equipped with cantilever scope mount rings; changeable choke tubes (rifled choke tube for slugs & improved cylinder choke tube)
Estimated Value: $295.00 - $375.00

**Remington Model 870 Youth Gun**
Same as the Model 870 Wingmaster Field except: 20 gauge only; 21" barrel with ventilated rib; lightweight; short stock; changeable choke tubes after 1985
Estimated Value: $160.00 - $200.00

**Remington Sportsman 12**

**Remington Model 870 Express**
**Gauge:** 12 magnum
**Action:** Slide action; hammerless; side ejection repeating
**Magazine:** 4-shot tubular
**Barrel:** 26" or 28" ventilated rib; "Rem Choke"
**Finish:** Blued; checkered hardwood semi-pistol grip stock & forearm
**Estimated Value: $160.00 - $200.00**

**Remington Sportsman 12 Pump**
**Gauge:** 12; regular or magnum
**Action:** Slide action; hammerless; side ejection; repeating
**Magazine:** 4-shot tubular
**Barrel:** 28" modified, 30" full; ventilated rib; "Rem Choke;" add 10% for "Rem Choke"
**Finish:** Blued; checkered walnut semi-pistol grip stock & slide handle; steel receiver; recoil pad
**Estimated Value: $200.00 - $250.00**

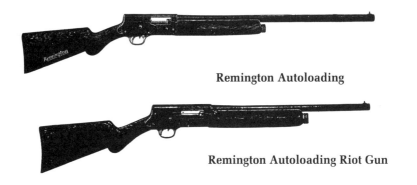

**Remington Autoloading**

**Remington Autoloading Riot Gun**

**Remington Autoloading Riot Gun**
Similar to the Autoloading Standard Grade except: 20" barrel
**Estimated Value: $200.00 - $250.00**

**Remington Autoloading**
**Gauge:** 12
**Action:** Semi-automatic; concealed hammer
**Magazine:** 5-shot tubular
**Barrel:** 26" or 28" steel; full, modified or cylinder bore
**Finish:** Blued; matted sight groove; plain or checkered straight or pistol grip stock & forearm; made in six grades; priced for Standard Grade
**Estimated Value: $210.00 - $260.00**

# Remington

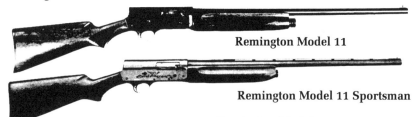

Remington Model 11

Remington Model 11 Sportsman

**Remington Model 11 Riot Gun**
Same as the Model 11 except; 20"
plain barrel
Estimated Value: $180.00 - $240.00

**Remington Model 11 Sportsman**
Same as the Model 11 except: 2-shot
magazine; made in six grades; priced
for the Standard Grade; add 10% for
solid or ventilated rib
Estimated Value: $250.00 - $325.00

**Remington Model 11**
**Gauge:** 12, 16, or 20
**Action:** Semi-automatic; concealed
hammer; side ejection; repeating
**Magazine:** 4-shot tubular
**Barrel:** 26", 28", 30", or 32"; full,
modified or cylinder choke; solid
or ventilated rib optional; add 10% for
ribbed barrel
**Finish:** Blued; wood semi-pistol grip
stock; straight grip on Trap grades;
checkering & fancy wood on higher
grades; made in six grades; priced
for Standard Grade
Estimated Value: $200.00 - $260.00

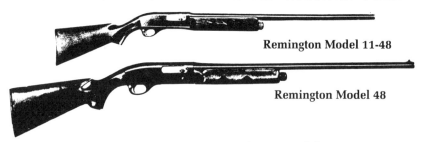

Remington Model 11-48

Remington Model 48

**Remington Model 11-48 Riot Gun**
Same general specifications as the
Model 11-48 except: 12 gauge only;
20" plain barrel
Estimated Value: $190.00 - $240.00

**Remington Model 48**
Similar to the Model 11-48 except:
2-shot magazine; 12, 16, or 20 gauge.
Made in several grades;  replaced
the Model 11 Sportsman; priced for
Standard Model;  add 10% for
ventilated rib
Estimated Value: $180.00 - $225.00

**Remington Model 11-48**
**Gauge:** 12, 16, 20, 28, or 410
**Action:** Semi-auto; hammerless; side
ejection; take down; cross bolt safety
**Magazine:** 4-shot tubular; 3-shot in
28 & 410 gauges
**Barrel:** 26", 28", or 30" in 12, 16, & 20
gauge; 25" in 28 & 410 bore; full, modified or improved cylinder choke; add
10% for optional ventilated rib
**Finish:** Checkered walnut pistol grip
stock with fluted comb, matching
semi-beavertail forearm;  higher
grades are fancier; made in about
seven grades; priced for Standard
model
Estimated Value: $215.00 - $265.00

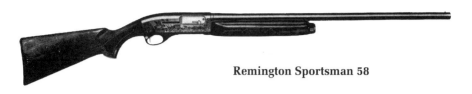

Remington Sportsman 58

**Remington Sportsman 58**
**Gauge:** 12, 16, or 20
**Action:** Semi-automatic; hammerless; side ejection; solid breech; gas operated sliding bolt; fixed barrel
**Magazine:** 2-shot tubular
**Barrel:** 26", 28", or 30"; plain or ventilated rib; add 10%for ventilated rib; full, modified, improved cylinder or skeet chokes
**Finish:** Blued; checkered walnut pistol grip stock with fluted comb & matching semi-beavertail forearm
**Estimated Value: $220.00 - $275.00**

**Remington Sportsman 58 Magnum**
Similar to the Sportsman 58 except: 12 gauge magnum; 30" barrel; recoil pad; add 10% for ventilated rib
**Estimated Value: $225.00 - $280.00**

**Remington Sportsman 58**
**Rifled Slug Special**
Same as the Sportsman 58 except: 12 gauge only; 26" barrel for slugs; equipped with rifle sights
**Estimated Value: $215.00 - $265.00**

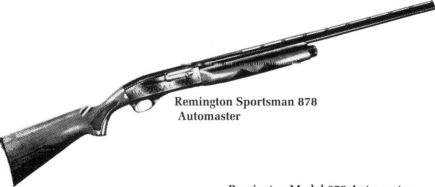

Remington Sportsman 878
Automaster

**Remington Sportsman 12 Auto**
**Gauge:** 12
**Action:** Gas operated semi-automatic
**Magazine:** 4-shot tubular
**Barrel:** 28" modified, 30" full; ventilated rib; "Rem Choke"optional; add 10% for "Rem Choke"
**Finish:** Checkered hardwood semi-pistol grip stock & forearm
**Estimated Value: $255.00 - $340.00**

**Remington Model 878 Automaster**
**Gauge:** 12
**Action:** Semi-auto; gas operated; hammerless
**Magazine:** 2-shot tubular
**Barrel:** 26"-30"; full, modified, improved cylinder or skeet chokes; plain barrel or ventilated rib; add 10% for ventilated rib
**Finish:** Blued; plain or checkered walnut pistol grip stock & forearm
**Estimated Value: $210.00 - $260.00**

# Remington

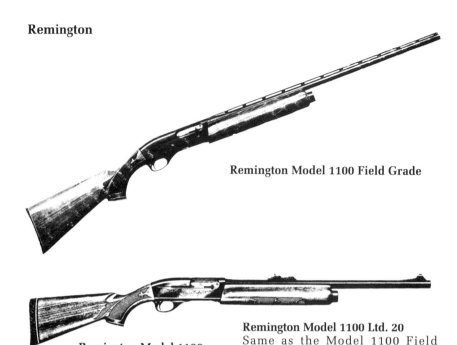

Remington Model 1100 Field Grade

Remington Model 1100 Deer Gun

**Remington Model 1100 Ltd. 20**
Same as the Model 1100 Field except: 20 gauge only; 23" ventilated rib barrel; lightweight
**Estimated Value: $320.00 - $400.00**

**Remington Model 1100 Youth Gun**
Same as the Model 1100 Field except: 20 gauge only; 21" ventilated rib barrel; lightweight; short stock; changeable choke tubes after 1985
**Estimated Value: $345.00 - $430.00**

**Remington Model 1100 Field Grade**
**Gauge:** 12, 16, 20, 28, or 410
**Action:** Semi-auto; gas operated sliding bolt; fixed barrel; solid breech; hammerless; takedown
**Magazine:** 4-shot tubular
**Barrel:** 26", 28" in 16 & 20 gauge; 26", 28", 30" in 12 gauge; 25" in 28 & 410; add 8% for gauges 28 or 410; full, modified, improved cylinder & skeet chokes; add 8% for optional "Rem Choke;" add 8% for optional ventilated rib
**Finish:** Blued; checkered wood pistol grip stock with fluted comb & matching forearm; engraved receiver; made in several grades; add 8% for left hand model
**Estimated Value: $350.00 - $440.00**

**Remington Model 1100 Magnum**
Similar to the Model 1100 Field except: 12 or 20 gauge magnum; 28" or 30" barrel; full or modified chokes; recoil pad; add 8% for left hand model
**Estimated Value: $320.00 - $400.00**

**Remington Model 1100 Deer Gun**
Similar to the Model 1100 Field except: 22" plain barrel & adjustable rifle sights; bored for rifled slugs; 12 or 20 gauge lightweight
**Estimated Value: $320.00 - $400.00**

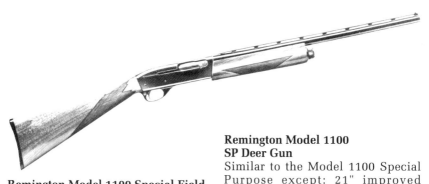

**Remington Model 1100 Special Field**

**Remington Model 1100
Special Purpose**
Similar to the Model 1100 Field except: oil-finished wood & Parkerized metal; recoil pad & nylon camo strap; 12 gauge only; ventilated rib barrel
Estimated Value: $345.00 - $460.00

**Remington Model 1100 Tournament Skeet**
Similar to the Model 1100 SA Skeet with higher quality finish
Estimated Value: $360.00 - $450.00

**Remington Model 1100
SP Deer Gun**
Similar to the Model 1100 Special Purpose except: 21" improved cylinder barrel & rifle sights
Estimated Value: $300.00 - $375.00

**Remington Model 1100 SA Skeet**
Similar to the Model 1100 Field except: 25" or 26" skeet choke barrel; ventilated rib; scroll receiver; add 8% for left hand model
Estimated Value: $340.00 - $425.00

**Remington Model 1100
Special Field**
Similar to the Model 1100 Field except: straight grip stock & 21" ventilated rib barrel; 12 or 20 gauge
Estimated Value: $350.00 - $440.00

**Remington Model 1100 Tournament Trap**

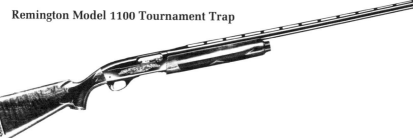

**Remington Model 1100
Tournament Trap**
Similar to the Model 1100 TA Trap with higher quality finish; add $10.00 for Monte Carlo stock
Estimated Value: $425.00 - $565.00

**Remington Model 1100 TA Trap**
Similar to the Model 1100 Field except: 30" full or modified trap barrel; ventilated rib; recoil pad; add $10.00 for optional Monte Carlo stock; add 8% for left hand model
Estimated Value: $360.00 - $475.00

# Remington

Remington Model 11-87 Premier

**Remington Model SP-10**
**Gauge:** 10
**Action:** Gas operated (non-corrosive stainless steel gas system) semi-automatic; safety in rear of trigger guard
**Magazine:** 3-shot tubular
**Barrel:** 26" or 30" matte, non-reflective blued finish with ventilated rib; full & modified choke tubes
**Finish:** Checkered walnut pistol grip stock & forearm with low gloss satin finish to reduce glare
**Estimated Value:** $560.00 - $700.00

**Remington Model 11-87 Premier**
**Gauge:** 12; regular & magnum
**Action:** Gas operated, semi-automatic
**Magazine:** 3-shot tubular
**Barrel:** 26", 28", or 30" with "Rem Choke"
**Finish:** Blued; checkered walnut pistol grip stock & forearm; add 8% for left hand model
**Estimated Value:** $365.00 - $455.00

**Remington Model 11-87**
**Premier Skeet**
Similar to the Model 11-87 Premier with 26" skeet or "Rem Choke" barrel; add 4% for "Rem Choke"
**Estimated Value:** $335.00 - $475.00

**Remington Model 11-87**
**Premier Trap**
Similar to the Model 11-87 Premier except: 30" barrel; full choke or "Rem Choke;" Monte Carlo or regular stock; add 4% for "Rem Choke" or Monte Carlo stock
**Estimated Value:** $400.00 - $500.00

**Remington Model 11-87**
**Special Purpose**
Similar to the Model 11-87 Premier with a 26" or 30" "Rem Choke" barrel, non-glare finish; recoil pad; ventilated rib; camo strap
**Estimated Value:** $360.00 - $450.00

**Remington Model 11-87 Cantilever**
Same as the Model 11-87 Special Purpose Deer Gun except: no sights; equipped with cantilever scope mount, rings & changeable choke tubes (rifled choke tube for slugs & improved cylinder tube)
**Estimated Value:** $375.00 - $465.00

**Remington Model 11-87 Special**
**Purpose Deer Gun**
Similar to the Model 11-87 Special Purpose except: 21" improved cylinder barrel & rifle sights
**Estimated Value:** $350.00 - $435.00

**118**

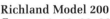

Richland Model 707 Deluxe

Richland Model 200

## Richland Model 200
**Gauge:** 12, 16, 20, 28, or 410
**Action:** Box lock; top lever, break-open; hammerless; double trigger
**Magazine:** None
**Barrel:** Double barrel (side by side); 22" improved cylinder & modified in 20 gauge; 26" or 28" improved & modified or modified & full chokes
**Finish:** Blued; checkered walnut pistol grip stock & tapered forearm; cheekpiece; recoil pad
**Estimated Value: $220.00 - $275.00**

## Richland Model 202
Same as the Model 200 except: extra set of barrels
**Estimated Value: $290.00 - $375.00**

## Richland Model 707 Deluxe
**Gauge:** 12 or 20
**Action:** Box lock; top lever, break-open; hammerless; double trigger
**Magazine:** None
**Barrel:** Double barrel (side by side); 26", 28", or 30"; variety of chokes
**Finish:** Blued; checkered walnut pistol grip stock & tapered forearm; recoil pad
**Estimated Value: $250.00 - $310.00**

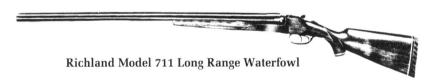

Richland Model 711 Long Range Waterfowl

## Richland Model 747
**Gauge:** 12 or 20, magnum
**Action:** Box lock; top lever, break-open; hammerless; single selective trigger
**Magazine:** None
**Barrel:** Over & under double barrel; 22" or 26" improved cylinder & modified, 28" modified & full
**Finish:** Blued; gray receiver; checkered walnut pistol grip stock & forearm; ventilated rib
**Estimated Value: $255.00 - $340.00**

## Richland Model 711 Long Range Waterfowl
**Gauge:** 10 or 12; magnum
**Action:** Box lock; top lever, break-open; hammerless; double trigger
**Magazine:** None
**Barrel:** Double barrel (side by side); 30" or 32" full choke
**Finish:** Blued; checkered walnut pistol grip stock & tapered forearm
**Estimated Value: $220.00 - $295.00**

# Richland

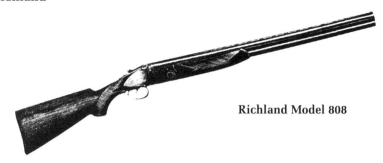

Richland Model 808

## Richland Model 808
**Gauge:** 12
**Action:** Box lock; top lever, break-open; hammerless; non-selective single trigger
**Magazine:** None
**Barrel:** Over & under double barrel; 26" improved cylinder & modified; 28" modified & full; 30" full & full; ventilated rib
**Finish:** Blued; checkered walnut pistol grip stock & forearm
**Estimated Value:** $300.00 - $375.00

## Richland Model 844
**Gauge:** 12; magnum
**Action:** Box lock; top lever, break-open; hammerless; non-selective single trigger
**Magazine:** None
**Barrel:** Over & under double barrel; 26" improved cylinder & modified; 28" modified & full; 30" full & full; ventilated rib
**Finish:** Blued; checkered walnut pistol grip stock & forearm
**Estimated Value:** $320.00 - $390.00

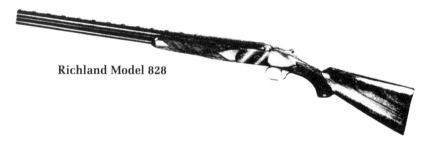

Richland Model 828

## Richland Model 828
**Gauge:** 28
**Action:** Box lock; top lever, break-open; hammerless
**Magazine:** None
**Barrel:** Over & under double barrel; 26" improved & modified; 28" modified & full chokes; ventilated rib
**Finish:** Blued; case hardened receiver; checkered walnut pistol grip stock & forearm
**Estimated Value:** $275.00 - $350.00

## Richland Model 41 Ultra
**Gauge:** 410
**Action:** Box lock; top lever, break-open; hammerless; single non-selective trigger
**Magazine:** None
**Barrel:** Over & under double barrel; 26" chrome lined, modified & full; ventilated rib
**Finish:** Blued; gray engraved receiver; checkered walnut pistol grip stock & forearm
**Estimated Value:** $200.00 - $275.00

# Ruger

**Ruger Over & Under "Red Label"**

### Ruger "Red Label" Sporting Clay
Similar to Ruger Over & Under Red Label except: 12 gauge only (3" chambers); 30" barrels; checkered walnut pistol grip stock and forearm; four screw-in chokes with each gun (modified, improved cylinder, and two skeet chokes)
**Estimated Value: $775.00 - $965.00**

### Ruger Over & Under "Red Label"
**Gauge:** 12 or 20 (3" chambers)
**Action:** Box lock; top lever, break-open; hammerless; single selective trigger
**Magazine:** None
**Barrel:** Over & under double barrel; 26" or 28" with a variety of screw-in chokes; ventilated rib;
**Finish:** Blued; stainless steel receiver on 12 gauge after 1985 and on 20 gauge after 1989; checkered walnut, straight or pistol grip stock & semi-beavertail forearm; recoil pad
**Estimated Value: $690.00 - $865.00**

# SKB

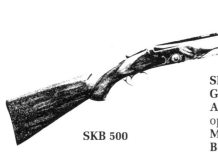

**SKB 500**

### SKB Model 505 Trap
Similar to the Model 505 except: 12 gauge only, 30" or 32" "Inter Choke" barrels
**Estimated Value: $710.00 - $885.00**

### SKB Model 500, 505F & 505CF
**Gauge:** 12 magnum, 20, 28, or 410
**Action:** Box lock; top lever, break-open; hammerless
**Magazine:** None
**Barrel:** Over & under double barrel; 26" improved cylinder & modified; 28" or 30" modified & full; ventilated rib; chrome lined; 505CF has "inter" choke system
**Finish:** Blued; checkered walnut pistol grip stock & forearm; recoil pad on magnum; engraved receiver on Model 500; Made from the mid-1960's to mid-1980's as Model 500; to present as model 505
**Estimated Value: $700.00 - $875.00**

# SKB

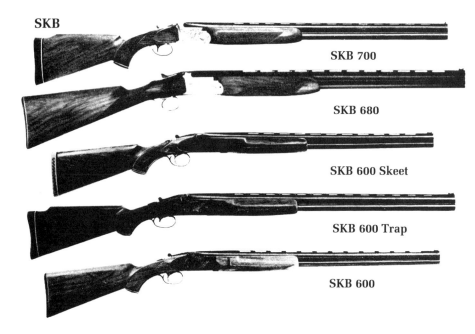

**SKB 700**

**SKB 680**

**SKB 600 Skeet**

**SKB 600 Trap**

**SKB 600**

**SKB Model 885**
Similar to the Model 505 except: engraved silver-plated receiver sideplates; add 3% for Trap or Skeet Model
**Estimated Value: $870.00 - $1,085.00**

**SKB Model 500 Skeet & 505 CSK**
Similar to the Model 500 except: 26" or 28" skeet choke barrels; Model 500 discontinued in mid-1980's & replaced by Model 505CSK
**Estimated Value: $730.00 - $915.00**

**SKB Model 600 Trap & 605 Trap**
Similar to the 600 except: regular or Monte Carlo stock; 12 gauge only; recoil pad, 30" or 32" full choke barrels on Model 600; "inter" choke system available on Model 605 Trap (late 1980's)
**Estimated Value: $950.00 - $1,195.00**

**SKB Model 600 & 605F**
Similar to the 500 except: select wood; trigger mounted barrel selector; silver-plate receiver
**Estimated Value: $585.00 - $730.00**

**SKB Model 600 Skeet & 605 CSK**
Similar to the 600 except: 26" or 28" skeet choke barrels (Model 600) & recoil pad; "inter" choke system on 605CSK (late 1980's)
**Estimated Value: $950.00 - $1,195.00**

**SKB Model 680**
Similar to the 600 except: a straight grip stock
**Estimated Value: $640.00 - $800.00**

**SKB Model 700**
Similar to the 600 except: higher quality finish & more extensive engraving
**Estimated Value: $680.00 - $850.00**

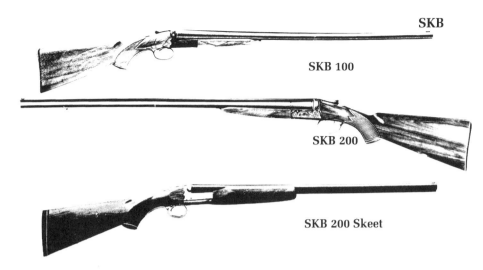

SKB 100

SKB 200

SKB 200 Skeet

**SKB Model 100**
**Gauge:** 12 or 20; magnum
**Action:** Box lock; top lever, break-open; hammerless; single selective trigger
**Magazine:** None
**Barrel:** Double barrel (side by side); 26" or 28" improved cylinder & modified or 30" full & full choke in 12 gauge
**Finish:** Blued; checkered hardwood pistol grip stock & short tapered forearm
**Estimated Value: $225.00 - $300.00**

**SKB Model 200 Skeet**
Similar to the 200 except: 25" skeet choke barrels & recoil pad
**Estimated Value: $420.00 - $525.00**

**SKB Model 200 & 200E**
Similar to the Model 100 except: engraved silver-plate receiver; wide forearm; select walnut; automatic selective ejectors; 200E has straight grip stock
**Estimated Value: $530.00 - $670.00**

SKB 280

**SKB Model 400**
Similar to the Model 200 & 200E except: sideplate receiver
**Estimated Value: $715.00 - $895.00**

**SKB Model 280**
Similar to the 200 except: without silver-plate receiver; straight grip stock
**Estimated Value: $375.00 - $500.00**

*Pocket Guide to Shotguns*

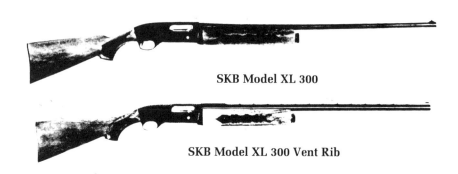

SKB Model XL 300

SKB Model XL 300 Vent Rib

**SKB Model 1300**
**Gauge:** 12 or 20; regular or magnum
**Action:** Semi-automatic
**Magazine:** 5-shot tubular
**Barrel:** 26" or 28" "Inter Choke;" ventilated rib; slug barrel with rifle sights optional
**Finish:** Blued, black receiver; checkered walnut pistol grip stock & forearm
**Estimated Value:** $430.00 - $540.00

**SKB Model 1900**
Similar to the Model 1300 except: light-weight receiver featuring engraved hunting scene; gold-plated trigger; add 5% for 30" barrel Trap Model
**Estimated Value:** $330.00 - $410.00

**SKB Model 3000**
A presentation deluxe version of the Model 1900; Highback receiver; add 2% for optional trap version
**Estimated Value:** $350.00 - $435.00

**SKB Model XL 300**
**Gauge:** 12 or 20
**Action:** Gas operated; semi-automatic; hammerless
**Magazine:** 5-shot tubular
**Barrel:** 26" improved cylinder or skeet; 28" modified or full; 30" modified or full chokes
**Finish:** Blued; decorated receiver; checkered walnut pistol grip stock & forearm
**Estimated Value:** $220.00 - $275.00

**SKB XL 300 Vent Rib**
Similar to the XL 300 except: ventilated rib
**Estimated Value:** $240.00 - $300.00

**SKB Model XL 100 Slug**
Similar to the Model XL 300; a no-frills slug gun with 20" barrel; rifle sights; swivels
**Estimated Value:** $175.00 - $235.00

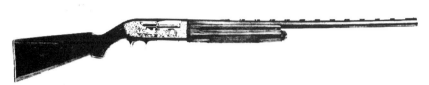

**SKB Model XL 900**

**SKB Model XL 900**
Similar to the XL 300 except:
Ventilated rib with engraved silver-plated receiver; gold-plated trigger
Estimated Value: $260.00 - $325.00

**SKB Model XL 900 Trap**
Similar to the XL 900 except:
without silver-plated receiver; recoil pad; choice of regular or Monte Carlo stock
Estimated Value: $280.00 - $350.00

**SKB Model XL 900 Slug**
Similar to the XL 900 except: 24" barrel for slugs; rifle sights; swivels
Estimated Value: $230.00 - $310.00

**SKB Model XL 900 Skeet**
Similar to the XL 900 Trap except: skeet stock & skeet choke barrel
Estimated Value: $250.00 - $330.00

**SKB Model XL 900 MR**
Similar to the XL 900 except: 3" magnum shells; recoil pad; deduct 10% for slug model
Estimated Value: $260.00 - $350.00

# Sarasqueta

**Sarasqueta Sidelock Grades 4 to 12**
**Gauge:** 12, 16, 20, or 28
**Action:** Side lock; top lever, break-open; hammerless; double triggers
**Magazine:** None
**Barrel:** Double barrel (side by side); standard barrel lengths & chokes to customer's specifications
**Finish:** Blued; checkered walnut straight or pistol grip stock & forearm; grades differ as to quality & extent of engraving
**Estimated Value:** $550.00 - $2,500.00

**Sarasqueta Sidelock**

### Sarasqueta/Sauer

**Sarasqueta Over & Under Deluxe**
**Gauge:** 12
**Action:** Side lock; top lever, break-open; hammerless; double triggers; automatic ejectors
**Magazine:** None
**Barrel:** Over & under double barrel; lengths & chokes made to customer's specifications
**Finish:** Blued; checkered walnut pistol grip stock & forearm
**Estimated Value: $850.00 - $1,200.00**

**Sarasqueta Model 2 & 3**
**Gauge:** 12, 16, 20, or 28
**Action:** Box lock; top lever, break-open; hammerless; double triggers
**Magazine:** None
**Barrel:** Double barrel (side by side); standard barrel lengths & chokes; as per customer's specifications
**Finish:** Blued; checkered walnut straight grip stock & forearm; grades differ only in engraving style
**Estimated Value: $325.00 - $550.00**

**Sarasqueta Folding Shotgun**
**Gauge:** 410
**Action:** Box lock; top lever, break-open; exposed hammer
**Magazine:** None
**Barrel:** Double barrel (side by side); 26" choice of chokes
**Finish:** Blued; case-hardened receiver; walnut pistol grip stock & forearm
**Estimated Value: $115.00 - $150.00**

**Sarasqueta Folding Shotgun**

# Sauer

**Sauer Royal**

**Sauer Royal**
**Gauge:** 12 or 20
**Action:** Box lock; top lever, break-open; hammerless; automatic ejectors; single selective trigger
**Magazine:** None
**Barrel:** Double barrel (side by side); 28" modified & full, 26" improved & modified in 20 gauge; 30" full in 12 gauge
**Finish:** Blued; engraved receiver; checkered walnut pistol grip stock & tapered forearm; recoil pad
**Estimated Value: $890.00 - $1,100.00**

Sauer Model 66 Field Grade

Sauer Model 66 Trap Grade

Sauer Model BBF

## Sauer Model 66 Field Grade
**Gauge:** 12
**Action:** Purdey action; hammerless; single selective trigger; automatic ejectors
**Magazine:** None
**Barrel:** Over & under double barrel; 28" modified & full choke; ventilated rib
**Finish:** Blued; checkered walnut pistol grip stock & forearm; recoil pad; engraving. Priced for Field grade. Grades II & III differ in quality & extent of engraving
**Estimated Value: $1,200.00 - $1,500.00**

## Sauer Model 66 Skeet
Basically the same as the Trap Model except: 25" barrels in skeet choke
**Estimated Value: $1,220.00 - $1,525.00**

## Sauer Model 66 Trap Grade
Basically the same as the Field Grade except: 30" barrels & a trap stock; produced in three grades
**Estimated Value: $1,240.00 - $1,550.00**

## Sauer Model BBF
**Gauge:** 16
**Caliber:** 30-30, 30-06, or 7 x 65
**Action:** Kersten lock; Blitz action; top lever, break-open; hammerless; double trigger
**Magazine:** None
**Barrel:** Over & under rifle-shotgun combination; 25" Krupp barrels; rifle barrel & full choke shotgun barrel
**Finish:** Blued; checkered walnut Monte Carlo pistol grip stock & forearm; engraved; sights; swivels; also available in deluxe model with extensive engraving
**Estimated Value: $1,200.00 - $1,600.00**

# Savage

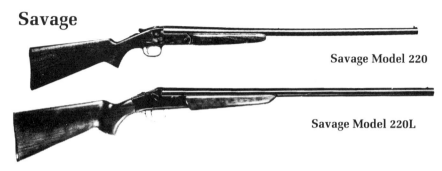

Savage Model 220

Savage Model 220L

**Savage Model 220P**
Basically the same as 220 except: no 410 gauge; "Poly-Choke" & recoil pad
**Estimated Value: $80.00 - $100.00**

**Savage Model 220L**
Similar to Model 220 except: side lever, break-open
**Estimated Value: $65.00 - $85.00**

**Savage Model 220**
**Gauge:** 12, 16, 20, 28, or 410
**Action:** Top lever, break-open; single shot; hammerless; automatic ejector
**Magazine:** None
**Barrel:** Full choke; 28", 30", 32" in 12 & 16 gauge; 26", 28", 30", 32" in 20 gauge; 28" & 30" in 28 gauge; 26" & 28" in 410 bore
**Finish:** Blued; plain wood, pistol grip stock & forearm
**Comments:** Made from 1930's until late 1940's; reintroduced in the mid-1950's with 36" barrel; replaced by 220L in mid-1960's
**Estimated Value: $70.00 - $90.00**

Savage Model 311

**Savage Model 311**
**Gauge:** 12 or 20; regular or magnum
**Action:** Top lever, break-open; hammerless, double trigger
**Magazine:** None
**Barrel:** Double barrel (side by side); 28" modified & full; matted rib
**Finish:** Blued; hardwood, semi-pistol grip stock & tapered forearm; the Model 311 was originally a Stevens shotgun; in 1988 Savage dropped the Stevens designation.
**Estimated Value: $185.00 - $230.00**

**Savage Model 311 Waterfowler**
Similar to the Model 311 with Parkerized finish
**Estimated Value: $185.00 - $230.00**

**Savage Model 242**

## Savage Model 24F Combination
**Gauge:** 20 or 12; 3" chamber
**Caliber:** 22 long rifle, 22 Hornet, 222 Rem., 223 Rem., 30-30 Win.
**Action:** Top lever, break open; exposed hammer with barrel selector; hammer block safety
**Magazine:** None
**Barrel:** 24" rifle barrel over 24" shotgun barrel; any combination of rifle caliber & shotgun gauge; shotgun barrel in modified choke; modified & full choke tubes optional; add 4% for choke tubes
**Finish:** DuPont Rynite® two-piece stock & forearm
**Estimated Value: $225.00 - $245.00**

## Savage Model 24V Combination
Same as the Model 24F Combination except: walnut finish hardwood stock & forearm; 20 gauge, 3" chamber under 222 Rem., 223 Rem., or 30-30 Win. rifle barrel
**Estimated Value: $200.00 - $250.00**

**Savage Model 24C Camper**

**Savage Model 24D**

## Savage Model 24D
Deluxe version of the Model 24
**Estimated Value: $160.00 - $200.00**

## Savage Model 24
**Gauge:** 20 or 410
**Caliber:** 22 short, long, long rifle; 22 magnum
**Action:** Top lever, break open; exposed hammer; single trigger with barrel slector
**Magazine:** None
**Barrel:** Over & under double barrel; 24" rifle barrel over shotgun barrel
**Finish:** Blued; checkered walnut finish hardwood pistol grip stock & forearm; sporting rear & ramp front sights; case hardened receiver
**Estimated Value: $145.00 - $180.00**

## Savage Model 24C Camper, 24CS
A shorter version of the Model 24 with a 20" barrel; 22LR over 20 gauge barrel; buttplate opens for ammo storage; add $45.00 for satin nickel finish (24CS) & extra pistol grip stock
**Estimated Value: $150.00 - $190.00**

## Savage Model 242
Similar to the Model 24 with 410 gauge over & under shotgun barrels; full choke; bead sights
**Estimated Value: $130.00 - $160.00**

# Savage

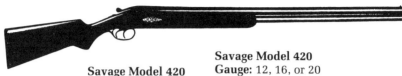

Savage Model 420

**Savage Model 389**
**Gauge:** 12; regular or magnum
**Caliber:** 222 or 308
**Action:** Top lever, break-open; hammerless; double trigger; shotgun barrel over rifle barrel; tang safety
**Magazine:** None
**Barrel:** 25¾" over & under double barrel; changeable choke tubes
**Finish:** Blued; checkered walnut pistol grip stock & forearm; sling studs
**Estimated Value: $550.00 - $670.00**

**Savage Model 420**
**Gauge:** 12, 16, or 20
**Action:** Box lock; top lever, break-open; hammerless; double triggers or non-selective single trigger; add $25.00 for single trigger
**Magazine:** None
**Barrel:** Over & under double barrel; 26" - 30" modified & full or cylinder bore & modified chokes
**Finish:** Blued; plain walnut pistol grip stock & forearm
**Estimated Value: $320.00 - $400.00**

**Savage Model 430**
Similar as Model 420 except: special checkered walnut stock & forearm; matted upper barrel; recoil pad; add $25.00 for single trigger
**Estimated Value: $360.00 - $450.00**

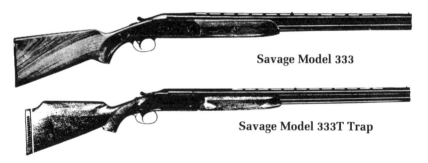

Savage Model 333

Savage Model 333T Trap

**Savage Model 333**
**Gauge:** 12 or 20
**Action:** Top lever, break-open; hammerless; single trigger
**Magazine:** None
**Barrel:** Over & under double barrel; 26" - 30"; variety of chokes; ventilated rib
**Finish:** Blued; checkered walnut pistol grip stock & forearm
**Estimated Value: $375.00 - $500.00**

**Savage Model 333T Trap**
Similar to 333 except: Monte Carlo stock; recoil pad; 12 gauge; 30" barrel
**Estimated Value: $395.00 - $525.00**

**Savage Model 330**
Similar to 333 except: no ventilated rib
**Estimated Value: $340.00 - $450.00**

**Savage Model 312 Field**
**Gauge:** 12; regular or magnum
**Action:** Top lever, break-open; concealed hammers; single trigger with safety acting as barrel selector
**Magazine:** None
**Barrel:** Over & under double barrel; 26" or 28"; ventilated rib; changeable choke tubes in full, modified, & improved cylinder
**Finish:** Blued; satin chrome receiver; cut-checkered walnut pistol grip stock & matching forearm; recoil pad
**Estimated Value: $325.00 - $405.00**

**Savage Model 320 Field**
Same as the Savage Model 312 Field except: 20 gauge (3" chambers) with 26" barrels
**Estimated Value: $325.00 - $405.00**

**Savage Model 312T**
Same as Model 312 Field except: 30" barrels; two full & one modified choke tubes; Monte Carlo stock
**Estimated Value: $345.00 - $430.00**

**Savage Model 312 SC**
Same as the Model 312 Field except: 28" barrels only; seven choke tubes included (one full, two improved cylinder, two modified, one #1 skeet & one #2 skeet); "Sporting Clays" engraved on receiver
**Estimated Value: $330.00 - $415.00**

Savage Model 28A

Savage Model 28D Trap

**Savage Model 28C Riot**
Basically the same as model 28A except: 20" cylinder bore barrel; used by police, bank guards, etc. for protection
**Estimated Value: $150.00 - $190.00**

**Savage Model 28D Trap**
Same as model 28B except: special straight grip checkered walnut stock and slide handle; 30" full choke barrel
**Estimated Value: $190.00 - $240.00**

**Savage Model 28A & B Standard**
**Gauge:** 12
**Action:** Slide action; hammerless; solid breech; side ejection
**Magazine:** 5-shot tubular
**Barrel:** 26", 28", 30", or 32" cylinder, modified or full choke; matted rib on 28B; add $10.00 for matted rib
**Finish:** Blued; checkered wood pistol grip stock & grooved slide handle
**Estimated Value: $175.00 - $220.00**

**Savage Model 28S Special**
Same as model 28B except: ivory bead front sight; checkered pistol grip stock and forearm
**Estimated Value: $180.00 - $225.00**

## Savage

Savage Model 30

Savage Model 30 FG

Savage Model 30 AC

Savage Model 30D

**Savage Model 30 FG Slug Gun**
Same as Model 30 FG except: 22"
barrel; rifle sights; 12 gauge
**Estimated Value: $140.00 - $175.00**

**Savage Model 30**
**Gauge:** 12, 20, or 410
**Action:** Slide action; hammerless
**Magazine:** 4-shot tubular
**Barrel:** 26", 28", or 30"; cylinder
bore, modified or full choke;
ventilated rib
**Finish:** Blued; decorated receiver;
walnut pistol grip stock & grooved
slide handle
**Estimated Value: $160.00 - $200.00**

**Savage Model 30 FG (Field Grade)**
Similar to Model 30 except: plain
receiver; no ventilated rib
**Estimated Value: $130.00 - $160.00**

**Savage Model 30 AC**
Same as Model 30 FG except:
adjustable choke
**Estimated Value: $135.00 - $170.00**

**Savage Model 30D (Deluxe)**
1970's version of the Model 30 with
recoil pad grooved slide handle
**Estimated Value: $130.00 - $175.00**

**Savage Model 30T Trap**
Fancy version of Model 30 in 12
gauge; 30" full choke barrel; Monte
Carlo stock; recoil pad
**Estimated Value: $165.00 - $210.00**

**Savage Model 69 RXL**

**Savage Model 67**
**Gauge:** 12 or 20; regular or magnum
**Action:** Slide action; hammerless; side ejecting; repeating
**Magazine:** 4-shot tubular, 3-shot in magnum
**Barrel:** 28"; modified
**Finish:** Blued; hardwood, semi-pistol grip stock & grooved slide handle; the Model 67 was originally a Stevens shotgun; in 1988 Savage dropped the Stevens designation.
**Estimated Value: $145.00 - $180.00**

**Savage Model 67 VRT**
Similar to the Model 67 except: ventilated rib; interchangeable choke tubes; recoil pad
**Estimated Value: $170.00 - $210.00**

**Savage Model 67 Slug**
Similar to Model 67 except: 21" cylinder bore barrel; recoil pad; rifle sights & scope mount
**Estimated Value: $150.00 - $195.00**

**Savage Model 69R, 69N, 69RXL, 69RXG**
**Gauge:** 12; regular or magnum
**Action:** Slide action; hammerless
**Magazine:** 6-shot tubular, 4-shot in 69R
**Barrel:** 18¼" cylinder bore; 20" on 69R
**Finish:** Blued; walnut stock & grooved slide handle; recoil pad, swivels; 69N has satin nickel finish; add 30% for satin nickel finish; 69RXG has plastic pistol grip & sling; a law enforcement gun introduced in 1982.
**Estimated Value: $145.00 - $190.00**

**Savage Model 720**

**Savage Model 720 P**
Same as Model 720 except: a "Poly-Choke"
**Estimated Value: $215.00 - $270.00**

**Savage Model 720**
**Gauge:** 12
**Action:** Browning patent; semi-automatic; hammerless
**Magazine:** 4-shot tubular
**Barrel:** 28", 30", or 32" cylinder bore, modified or full choke; in the early 1940's Model 720R (Riot Gun) was introduced with a 20" barrel.
**Finish:** Blued; checkered walnut pistol grip stock & forearm; engraved receiver, after 1940
**Estimated Value: $210.00 - $265.00**

# Savage

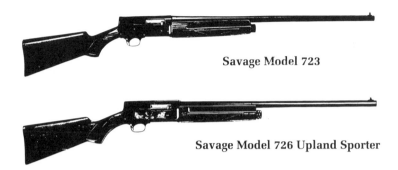

Savage Model 723

Savage Model 726 Upland Sporter

**Savage Model 721**
Same as Model 720 except: matted rib
Estimated Value: $220.00 - $275.00

**Savage Model 723**
Same as Model 720 except: 28" or 30" barrel; 12 or 16 gauge
Estimated Value: $205.00 - $260.00

**Savage Model 722**
Same as Model 720 except: ventilated rib
Estimated Value: $230.00 - $290.00

**Savage Model 724**
Same as Model 723 except: matted rib
Estimated Value: $220.00 - $275.00

**Savage Model 725**
Same as Model 723 except: ventilated rib
Estimated Value: $230.00 - $290.00

**Savage Model 726 Upland Sporter**
Basically the same as Model 720 except: 28" or 30" barrel; 2-shot tubular magazine; 12 or 16 gauge; decorated receiver
Estimated Value: $220.00 - $275.00

**Savage Model 727 Upland Sporter**
Same as Model 726 Upland Sporter except: matted rib
Estimated Value: $230.00 - $285.00

**Savage Model 728 Upland Sporter**
Same as Model 726 Upland Sporter except: ventilated rib
Estimated Value: $240.00 - $300.00

**Savage Model 740C Skeet Gun**
Basically the same as Model 726 Upland Sporter except: skeet stock & "Cutts Compensator"
Estimated Value: $225.00 - $280.00

**Savage Model 745 Lightweight**
Similar to Model 720 except: light alloy receiver
Estimated Value: $210.00 - $260.00

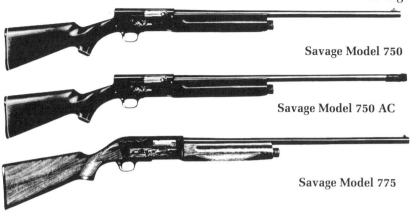

Savage Model 750

Savage Model 750 AC

Savage Model 775

Savage Model 775 - SC

**Savage Model 750**
**Gauge:** 12
**Action:** Browning patent; semi-automatic; hammerless
**Magazine:** 4-shot tubular
**Barrel:** 26" cylinder bore; 28" full or modified
**Finish:** Blued; checkered walnut pistol grip stock & forearm; decorated receiver
**Estimated Value: $240.00 - $300.00**

**Savage Model 750 SC**
Same as Model 750 except: Savage "Super Choke"
**Estimated Value: $250.00 - $310.00**

**Savage Model 750 AC**
Same as Model 750 except: adjustable choke
**Estimated Value: $220.00 - $275.00**

**Savage Model 755**
**Gauge:** 12 or 16
**Action:** Semi-automatic; hammerless
**Magazine:** 4-shot tubular; 3-shot tubular
**Barrel:** 26" cylinder bore; 28" full or modified; 30" full choke
**Finish:** Blued; checkered walnut pistol grip stock & forearm
**Estimated Value: $195.00 - $240.00**

**Savage Model 755 - SC**
Same as Model 755 except: Savage "Super Choke"
**Estimated Value: $200.00 - $250.00**

**Savage Model 775 Lightweight**
Same as Model 755 except: alloy receiver
**Estimated Value: $190.00 - $235.00**

**Savage Model 775 - SC**
Basically the same as Model 775 Lightweight except: Savage "Super Choke;" 26" barrel
**Estimated Value: $200.00 - $245.00**

# Sears

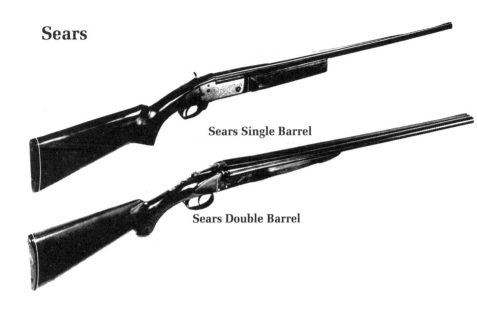

Sears Single Barrel

Sears Double Barrel

**Sears Single Barrel**
**Gauge:** 12, 20, or 410
**Action:** Box lock; top lever, break-open; exposed hammer; automatic ejector
**Magazine:** None
**Barrel:** 26" in 410 ga.; 28" in 20 ga.; 30" in 12 ga.; full choke
**Finish:** Blued; wood pistol grip stock & forearm
**Estimated Value: $65.00 - $80.00**

**Sears Double Barrel**
**Gauge:** 12 or 20
**Action:** Box lock; top lever, break-open; hammerless; double triggers
**Magazine:** None
**Barrel:** Double barrel (side by side); 28"; variety of chokes
**Finish:** Blued; epoxied black frame; walnut pistol grip stock & forearm
**Estimated Value: $160.00 - $200.00**

Sears Ted Williams Over & Under

**Sears Ted Williams Over & Under**
**Gauge:** 12 or 20
**Action:** Box lock; top lever, break-open; hammerless; automatic ejectors, selective trigger
**Magazine:** None
**Barrel:** Over & under double barrel; 26" or 28" in standard chokes; ventilated rib; chrome lined barrel
**Finish:** Blued; engraved steel receiver; checkered walnut pistol grip stock & forearm; recoil pad
**Estimated Value: $320.00 - $400.00**

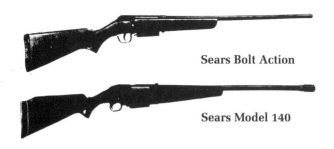

Sears Bolt Action

Sears Model 140

**Sears Bolt Action**
**Gauge:** 410
**Action:** Bolt action; repeating
**Magazine:** 3-shot detachable clip
**Barrel:** 24"; full choke
**Finish:** Blued; wood pistol grip stock & forearm
**Estimated Value:** $75.00 - $95.00

**Sears Model 140**
**Gauge:** 12 or 20
**Action:** Bolt action; repeating
**Magazine:** 2-shot detachable clip
**Barrel:** 25"; adjustable choke
**Finish:** Blued; wood pistol grip stock & forearm
**Estimated Value:** $70.00 - $90.00

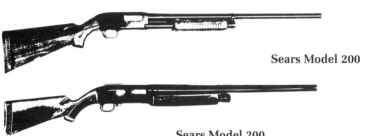

Sears Model 200

Sears Ted Williams 200

**Sears Ted Williams 300**
**Gauge:** 12 or 20
**Action:** Semi-auto, gas operated; hammerless
**Magazine:** 3-shot tubular
**Barrel:** 28" modified or full choke; 27" adjustable choke; add 5% for variable choke; ventilated rib
**Finish:** Blued; checkered walnut pistol grip stock & forearm; recoil pad
**Estimated Value:** $200.00 - $250.00

**Sears Model 200**
**Gauge:** 12 or 20
**Action:** Slide action; hammerless; repeating
**Magazine:** 4-shot tubular
**Barrel:** 28"; full or modified choke; add 10% for variable choke
**Finish:** Blued; alloy receiver; wood pistol grip stock & forearm; recoil pad
**Estimated Value:** $140.00 - $175.00

**Sears Ted Williams 200**
A fancier version of the Model 200 with checkered wood
**Estimated Value:** $160.00 - $200.00

# Smith & Wesson

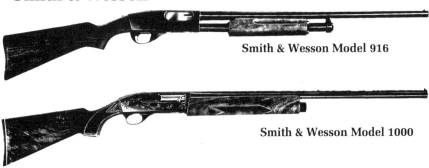

Smith & Wesson Model 916

Smith & Wesson Model 1000

## Smith & Wesson Model 916
**Gauge:** 12
**Action:** Slide action; hammerless; side ejection
**Magazine:** 5-shot tubular
**Barrel:** Add 10% for 20" cylinder bore; 26" improved cylinder, 28" modified, full or cylinder bore; add 10% for optional ventilated rib
**Finish:** Blued; satin finish receiver; walnut semi-pistol grip stock & grooved slide handle; recoil pad
**Estimated Value: $140.00 - $175.00**

## Smith & Wesson Model 1000
**Gauge:** 12 or 20; regular or magnum; add 10% for magnum
**Action:** Semi-automatic, gas operated; hammerless; side ejection
**Magazine:** 3-shot tubular
**Barrel:** 26", 28", or 30"; variety of chokes; add 10% for "Multi-Choke" system; ventilated rib
**Finish:** Blued; engraved alloy receiver; steel receiver on magnum; checkered walnut pistol grip stock & forearm; sights
**Estimated Value: $285.00 - $380.00**

## Smith & Wesson Model 1000 Super 12
Similar to the Model 1000 except: "Multi-Choke" system; designed to use magnum shells
**Estimated Value: $335.00 - $450.00**

## Smith & Wesson Model 1000 Trap
Similar to the Model 1000 except: Monte Carlo stock; steel receiver; 30" multi-choke barrel; other trap features
**Estimated Value: $340.00 - $450.00**

## Smith & Wesson Model 1000 Slug
Similar to the Model 1000 except: 22" slug barrel; rifle sights & steel receiver
**Estimated Value: $285.00 - $380.00**

## Smith & Wesson Model 1000S, Superskeet
Similar to the Model 1000 except: 25" skeet choke barrel; muzzle vents & other extras; add 50% for Superskeet Model
**Estimated Value: $320.00 - $400.00**

## Smith & Wesson Model 1000 Waterfowler
Similar to the Model 1000 except: steel receiver; dull oil-finish stock; 30" full choke barrel; Parkerized finish; swivels; recoil pad; camouflage sling
**Estimated Value: $325.00 - $435.00**

## Smith & Wesson Model 1000 Super 12 Waterfowler
Similar to the Model 1000 Waterfowler except: "Multi-Choke" system
**Estimated Value: $350.00 - $470.00**

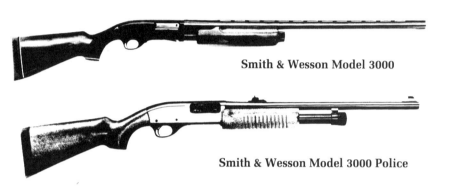

Smith & Wesson Model 3000

Smith & Wesson Model 3000 Police

## Smith & Wesson Model 3000
**Gauge:** 12 or 20; regular or magnum
**Action:** Slide action; repeating; hammerless
**Magazine:** 3-shot tubular
**Barrel:** 26" improved cylinder; 28" modified or full; 30" full; add 10% for "Multi-Choke" system; ventilated rib
**Finish:** Blued; checkered walnut pistol grip stock & fluted slide handle; recoil pad
**Estimated Value: $225.00 - $300.00**

## Smith & Wesson Model 3000 Slug
Similar to the Model 3000 except: 22" slug barrel; rifle sights; swivels
**Estimated Value: $200.00 - $270.00**

## Smith & Wesson Model 3000 Waterfowler
Similar to the Model 3000 except: steel receiver; 30" full choke barrel; Parkerized finish; dull, oil-finished wood; camouflaged sling & swivels; add $25.00 for "Multi-Choke" system
**Estimated Value: $240.00 - $320.00**

## Smith & Wesson Model 3000 Police
Similar to the Model 3000 except: 18" or 20" slug or cylinder bore barrel; blued or Parkerized finish; bead or rifle sights; walnut finish, hardwood stock & grooved slide handle; or plastic pistol grip & slide handle; or folding stock; add 10% for rifle sights; add 5% for plastic pistol grip and slide handle; add 25% folding stock
**Estimated Value: $185.00 - $250.00**

# Stevens

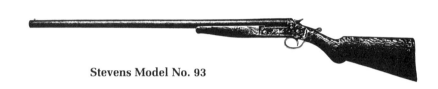

Stevens Model No. 93

**Stevens Models No. 93, 97 Nitro Special**
**Gauge:** 12 or 16
**Action:** Top lever, break-open; exposed hammer; single shot
**Magazine:** None, single shot
**Barrel:** Special steel; 28", 30", or 32"
**Finish:** Blued or nickel plated, case hardened receiver; plain walnut pistol grip stock & lipped forearm
**Estimated Value: $60.00 - $80.00**

Stevens Model No. 97 Nitro Special

**Stevens Models No. 100, 110, & 120**
**Gauge:** 12, 16, or 20
**Action:** Top lever, break-open; automatic ejector; exposed hammer; single shot
**Magazine:** None
**Barrel:** 28", 30", or 32"
**Finish:** Blued; case hardened receiver; walnut pistol grip stock & forearm; No. 100 no checkering; 110 & 120 checkered walnut
**Estimated Value: $65.00 - $85.00**

Stevens Model No. 120

**Stevens Model No. 140**
Similar to the Model 120 except: hammerless & has an automatic safety
**Estimated Value: $85.00 - $110.00**

Stevens Model No. 140

**Stevens Model No. 170**

**Stevens Model No. 180**

**Stevens Model No. 182 Trap Gun**
Similar to Model No. 180 except:
Trap Grade; 12 gauge only; matted
top of barrel; scroll work on frame
Estimated Value: $110.00 - $150.00

**Stevens Models No. 160, 165, or 170**
**Gauge:** 12, 16, or 20
**Action:** Break-open; exposed
hammer; single shot; automatic
ejector except on 160
**Magazine:** None; single shot
**Barrel:** 26", 28", 30", or 32"
**Finish:** Blued; case hardened
receiver; checkered walnut pistol
grip stock & forearm except 160,
which is plain
Estimated Value: $60.00 - $80.00

**Stevens Model No. 180**
**Gauge:** 12, 16, or 20
**Action:** Top lever, break-open;
hammerless; automatic ejector
**Magazine:** None; single shot
**Barrel:** 26", 28", or 30" modified; 32"
or 36" full choke
**Finish:** Blued; case hardened
receiver; checkered walnut pistol
grip stock & forearm
Estimated Value: $80.00 - $100.00

**Stevens Model No. 182 Trap Gun**

**Stevens Model No. 185, 190, 195**
**Gauge:** 12
**Action:** Top lever, break-open;
hammerless; automatic shell ejector;
single shot
**Magazine:** None
**Barrel:** Round with octagon breech;
30" or 32"
**Finish:** Blued; case hardened frame;
checkered walnut pistol grip stock &
forearm; receiver engraved on No.
190 & 195
Estimated Value: $110.00 - $150.00

**Stevens Model No. 195**

**Stevens Model No. 970**
Similar to the 185; a 12 gauge made
from around 1912 to 1918
Estimated Value: $70.00 - $90.00

**Stevens Model No. 970**

# Stevens

Stevens Model No. 85 Dreadnaught

**Stevens Model No. 85 Dreadnaught**
**Gauge:** 12
**Action:** Top lever, break-open; exposed hammer
**Magazine:** None, single shot
**Barrel:** 28", 30", or 32"; full choke
**Finish:** Blued; case hardened receiver; plain walnut pistol grip stock & lipped forearm
**Estimated Value: $65.00 - $80.00**

**Stevens Model No. 89 Dreadnaught**
Same as the No. 85 except: automatic ejector
**Estimated Value: $70.00 - $85.00**

Stevens Model No. 89 Dreadnaught

Stevens Model No. 106

**Stevens Model No. 106**
**Gauge:** 410
**Action:** Top lever, break-open; exposed hammer; single shot
**Magazine:** None
**Barrel:** 26" or 30"
**Finish:** Blued; case hardened receiver; plain walnut pistol grip stock & forearm
**Estimated Value: $60.00 - $80.00**

**Stevens Model No. 108**
Same as the No. 106 except: automatic ejector
**Estimated Value: $65.00 - $85.00**

**Stevens Springfield Model No. 958**
Similar to Model No. 108; made from mid-1920's to early 1930's
**Estimated Value: $60.00 - $80.00**

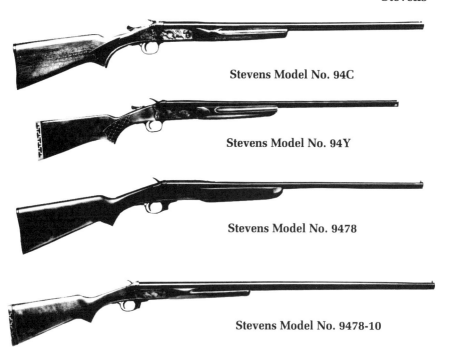

Stevens Model No. 94C

Stevens Model No. 94Y

Stevens Model No. 9478

Stevens Model No. 9478-10

### Stevens Model No. 94, 94C
**Gauge:** 12, 16, 20, or 410
**Action:** Top lever, break-open; exposed hammer
**Magazine:** None; single shot
**Barrel:** 26", 28", 30", 32", or 36"; full choke
**Finish:** Blued; case hardened receiver; checkered or plain walnut semi-pistol grip stock & grooved forearm
**Estimated Value: $65.00 - $85.00**

### Stevens Model No. 94Y
Similar to 94C except: youth version; shorter stock; recoil pad; 26" barrel; 20 gauge modified or 410 full choke
**Estimated Value: $60.00 - $80.00**

### Stevens Model No. 9478
Similar to the Model 94C except: lever release on the trigger guard; no checkering; add 10% for 36" barrel
**Estimated Value: $60.00 - $80.00**

### Stevens Model No. 9478-10, Waterfowl
Similar to the Model 9478 except: 10 gauge only; 36" full choke barrel; recoil pad
**Estimated Value: $80.00 - $100.00**

### Stevens Model No. 9478-Y
Similar to the Model 9478 except: 410 full or 20 modified gauges; 26" barrel; short stock with rubber buttplate
**Estimated Value: $65.00 - $80.00**

**Stevens**

**Stevens Models No. 105, 107, 115, & 125**
**Gauge:** 12, 16, 20, or 28
**Action:** Top lever, break-open; exposed hammer; single shot; automatic ejector on all except Model 105
**Magazine:** None, single shot
**Barrel:** 26" or 28"
**Finish:** Blued; case hardened receiver; checkered or plain walnut semi-pistol grip stock & forearm
**Estimated Value: $70.00 - $85.00**

**Stevens Model No. 125**

**Stevens Springfield Model No. 95**
Similar to the Model 107 with plain stock and forearm
**Estimated Value: $60.00 - $80.00**

Stevens Model No. 107

Stevens Model No. 115

**Stevens Models No. 116 & 117**
Similar to the Model 115 with automatic ejector. Model No. 117 is equipped with Lyman sights
**Estimated Value: $70.00 - $90.00**

Stevens Model No. 116

**144**

**Stevens Models No. 235, 255, & 265**
**Gauge:** 12 or 16
**Action:** Box lock; top lever, break-open; exposed hammers; double triggers
**Magazine:** None
**Barrel:** Double barrel (side by side); 28", 30, or 32"; matted rib
**Finish:** Blued; checkered walnut pistol grip stock & forearm; case hardened receiver
**Estimated Value:** $160.00 - $210.00

**Stevens Model No. 235**

**Stevens Model No. 255**

**Stevens Model No. 250**

**Stevens Model No. 250**
**Gauge:** 12
**Action:** Top lever, break-open; exposed hammer; double trigger
**Magazine:** None
**Barrel:** double barrel (side by side); 28", 30", or 32"
**Finish:** Blued; checkered walnut pistol grip stock & forearm
**Estimated Value:** $165.00 - $225.00

**Stevens Model No. 350**

**Stevens Models No. 260 & 270**
Similar to Model 250 except: special Damascus or twist barrels; 12 or 16 gauge
**Estimated Value:** $150.00 - $200.00

**Stevens Models No. 350, 360, & 370**
**Gauge:** 12 or 16
**Action:** Top lever, break-open; hammerless; double trigger
**Magazine:** None
**Barrel:** Double barrel (side by side); matted rib, 28", 30", or 32"
**Finish:** Blued; checkered walnut pistol grip stock & forearm
**Estimated Value:** $140.00 - $180.00

## Stevens

**Stevens Models No. 355, 365, 375, & 385**
**Gauge:** 12 or 16
**Action:** Top lever, break-open; hammerless; double trigger
**Magazine:** None
**Barrel:** Double barrel (side by side); Krupp steel; matted rib; 28", 30", or 32"
**Finish:** Blued; checkered walnut straight or pistol grip stock & forearm; 355 & 365 plain; 375 some engraving; 385 engraved receiver
**Estimated Value:** $150.00 - $200.00

Stevens Model No. 355

Stevens Model No. 385

**Stevens Riverside Model No. 215**
**Gauge:** 12 or 16
**Action:** Top lever, break-open; exposed hammer; double trigger
**Magazine:** None
**Barrel:** Double barrel (side by side); 26", 28", 30", or 32"; full and modified choke; matted rib
**Finish:** Blued; case hardened receiver; checkered walnut pistol grip stock & forearm
**Estimated Value:** $150.00 - $200.00

Stevens Riverside Model No. 215

Stevens Riverside Model No. 315

**Stevens Riverside Model No. 315**
**Gauge:** 12 or 16
**Action:** Top lever, break-open; hammerless; double trigger
**Magazine:** None
**Barrel:** Double barrel (side by side); 26", 28", 30", or 32"; full and modified choke; matted rib
**Finish:** Blued; case hardened receiver; checkered walnut semi-pistol grip stock & forearm
**Estimated Value:** $150.00 - $195.00

Stevens Model No. 335

Stevens Model No. 345

**Stevens Model No. 335**
Similar to the 315; produced from around 1912 to 1930
**Estimated Value:** $135.00 - $180.00

**Stevens Model No. 345**
Similar to the No. 335 except: 20 gauge
**Estimated Value:** $150.00 - $200.00

**Stevens Model No. 330**

**Stevens Model No. 330**
**Gauge:** 12, 16, 20, or 410
**Action:** Top lever, break-open; hammerless; double trigger; takedown model
**Magazine:** None
**Barrel:** Double barrel (side by side); 26"-32"; modified and full choke; full choke in 410
**Finish:** Blued; case hardened receiver; checkered black walnut pistol grip stock & forearm
**Estimated Value: $140.00 - $185.00**

**Stevens Model No. 311**

**Model No. 315**

**Stevens Model 311-R**

**Stevens Springfield Model No. 315**
A higher quality version of the Model 311
**Estimated Value: $190.00 - $240.00**

**Stevens Model 311-R**
A law enforcement version of the Model 311 with 18¼" cylinder bore barrel; recoil pad; 12 gauge only
**Estimated Value: $175.00 - $220.00**

**Stevens Model 311,**
**Stevens Springfield Model No. 311**
**Springfield Hammerless**
**Gauge:** 12, 16, 20, or 410
**Action:** Top lever, break-open; hammerless; double trigger; or single selective trigger; add 10% for single selective trigger; takedown model
**Magazine:** None
**Barrel:** Double barrel (side by side); 24"-32"; modified and full choke; except 32" 12 gauge is full choke & 410 ga. full choke; matted rib
**Finish:** Blued; case hardened receiver; smooth walnut semi-pistol grip stock & forearm
**Estimated Value: $180.00 - $225.00**

# Stevens

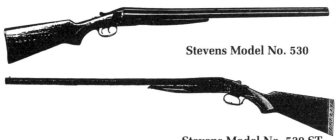

Stevens Model No. 530

Stevens Model No. 530 ST

Model No. 530M

Stevens Model 511

**Stevens Model No. 530 ST**
Same as 530 except: non-selective single trigger
**Estimated Value: $160.00 - $200.00**

**Stevens Model No. 530M**
Same as 530 except: plastic stock
**Estimated Value: $120.00 - $160.00**

**Stevens Model No. 530**
**Gauge:** 12, 16, 20, or 410
**Action:** Box lock; top lever, break-open; hammerless; double trigger
**Magazine:** None
**Barrel:** Double barrel (side by side); 26"-32"; modified and full choke; except 32" 12 gauge is full choke & 410 ga. full choke
**Finish:** Blued; case hardened frame; checkered walnut pistol grip stock & forearm; recoil pad on early model
**Estimated Value: $155.00 - $195.00**

**Stevens Model 511**
**Gauge:** 12 or 20; regular or magnum
**Action:** Box lock; top lever, break-open; double trigger
**Magazine:** None
**Barrel:** Double barrel (side by side); 28" modified & full choke
**Finish:** Blued; checkered hardwood semi-pistol grip stock & small forearm; case hardened receiver
**Estimated Value: $150.00 - $200.00**

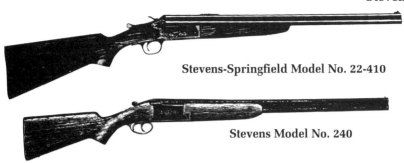

Stevens-Springfield Model No. 22-410

Stevens Model No. 240

**Stevens Model No. 240**
**Gauge:** 410
**Action:** Top lever, break-open;
exposed hammer; double trigger;
takedown
**Magazine:** None
**Barrel:** Over & under double barrel;
both barrels 26" full choke
**Finish:** Blued; checkered plastic or
wood pistol grip stock & forearm
**Estimated Value: $260.00 - $320.00**

**Stevens-Springfield**
**Model No. 22-410**
**Gauge:** 410 & 22 caliber rifle
**Action:** Top lever, break-open;
exposed hammer; single trigger;
separate extractors
**Magazine:** None
**Barrel:** 24" Over & under double
barrel; 22 rifle over 410 shotgun
**Finish:** Blued; case hardened
receiver; plastic semi-pistol grip
stock & forearm; open rear, ramp
front sight
**Estimated Value: $110.00 - $140.00**

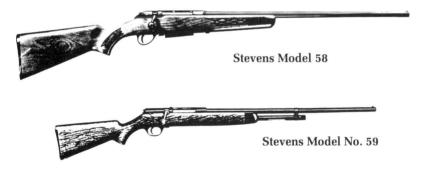

Stevens Model 58

Stevens Model No. 59

**Stevens Model No. 59**
Similar to No. 58 except: 5-shot
tubular magazine
**Estimated Value: $80.00 - $100.00**

**Stevens Model No. 58**
**Gauge:** 410
**Action:** Bolt-action
**Magazine:** 3-shot detachable box
**Barrel:** 24"; full choke
**Finish:** Blued; plain or walnut one-
piece pistol grip stock & forearm
**Estimated Value: $65.00 - $85.00**

# Stevens

Stevens-Springfield Model 38

Stevens-Springfield Model 39

**Stevens-Springfield Model 38**
Similar to Stevens Model No. 58;
made 1939 to 1947
**Estimated Value: $65.00 - $80.00**

**Stevens-Springfield Model 39**
Similar to Stevens Model No. 59;
made 1939 to 1947
**Estimated Value: $70.00 - $90.00**

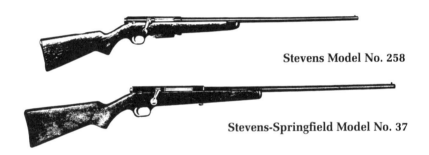

Stevens Model No. 258

Stevens-Springfield Model No. 37

**Stevens Model No. 258**
**Gauge:** 20
**Action:** Bolt action; repeating
**Magazine:** 2-shot detachable box
**Barrel:** 26"; full choke
**Finish:** Blued; plain walnut one-piece pistol grip stock & forearm
**Estimated Value: $65.00 - $85.00**

**Stevens Model No. 254**
A single shot version of the Model 258
**Estimated Value: $50.00 - $65.00**

**Stevens-Springfield Model 238**
Similar to Stevens Model 258; made 1939 to 1947
**Estimated Value: $70.00 - $90.00**

**Stevens-Springfield Model 237**
Similar to Stevens Model No. 254; made from 1939 to 1942
**Estimated Value: $55.00 - $70.00**

**Stevens-Springfield Model No. 37**
Similar to Stevens-Springfield Model 237 except: 410 bore; made from 1939 to 1942
**Estimated Value: $60.00 - $75.00**

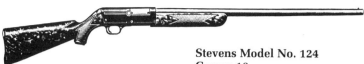

**Stevens Model No. 124**

**Stevens Model No. 124**
**Gauge:** 12
**Action:** Semi-automatic; side ejection; hammerless
**Magazine:** 2-shot tubular
**Barrel:** 28"; improved cylinder, modified or full choke
**Finish:** Blued; checkered plastic pistol grip stock & forearm
**Estimated Value: $100.00 - $125.00**

**Stevens Model No. 520**

**Stevens Model No. 522**

**Stevens Model No. 525**

**Stevens Models No. 520, 521, & 522**
**Gauge:** 12
**Action:** Browning patent; slide action; takedown; side ejection; hammerless
**Magazine:** 5-shot tubular
**Barrel:** 26"-32"; full, modified, or cylinder choke; matted rib on 521
**Finish:** Blued; walnut pistol grip stock & grooved slide handle; checkered straight grip & slide handle on 522
**Estimated Value: $145.00 - $180.00**

**Stevens Model No. 535**

**Stevens Models No. 525, 530, & 535**
Similar to 520 except fancier grades; 525 is custom built; 530 custom built with engraved receiver & rib; 535 custom built, heavily engraved; add 30% for engraving
**Estimated Value: $170.00 - $225.00**

# Stevens

Stevens Model No. 200

Stevens Model No. 620

Stevens Model No. 620-P

## Stevens Model No. 620
**Gauge:** 12, 16, or 20
**Action:** Slide action; hammerless; side ejection; take down model
**Magazine:** 5-shot tubular
**Barrel:** 26"-32"; full, modified, or cylinder bore
**Finish:** Blued; checkered walnut pistol grip stock & slide handle
**Estimated Value: $140.00 - $185.00**

## Stevens Model No. 200
**Gauge:** 20
**Action:** Pedersen patent, slide action; hammerless; side ejection; takedown
**Magazine:** 5-shot tubular
**Barrel:** 26"-32"; full , modified, or cylinder bore
**Finish:** Blued; walnut pistol grip stock & grooved slide handle
**Estimated Value: $150.00 - $190.00**

## Stevens Model No. 620-P
Same as Model No. 620 with"Poly-Choke"
**Estimated Value: $150.00 - $190.00**

## Stevens Model No. 621
Same as Model No. 620 except: matted rib
**Estimated Value: $150.00 - $195.00**

Stevens Model No. 77

## Stevens Model No. 77-SC
Same as No. 77 except: Savage "Super Choke" & recoil pad
**Estimated Value: $150.00 - $190.00**

## Stevens Model No. 77
**Gauge:** 12 or 16
**Action:** Slide action; hammerless; side ejection
**Magazine:** 5-shot tubular
**Barrel:** 26" or 28"; improved cylinder, modified or full choke
**Finish:** Blued; plain walnut pistol grip stock & grooved slide handle
**Estimated Value: $145.00 - $180.00**

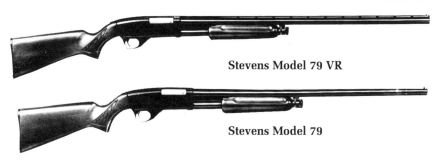

Stevens Model 79 VR

Stevens Model 79

**Stevens Model 79 VR**
Similar to the Model 79 except:
ventilated rib
**Estimated Value: $150.00 - $190.00**

**Stevens Model 79 Slug**
Similar to the Model 79 except: 21"
slug barrel; rifle sights
**Estimated Value: $140.00 - $175.00**

**Stevens Model No. 79**
**Gauge:** 12, 20, or 410; regular or
magnum
**Action:** Slide action; hammerless;
side ejection, repeating
**Magazine:** 4-shot tubular; 3-shot in
magnum
**Barrel:** 28" modified or 30" full in 12
gauge; 28" modified or full in 20
gauge; 26" full in 410
**Finish:** Blued; checkered hardwood
semi-pistol grip stock & fluted slide
handle
**Estimated Value: $135.00 - $170.00**

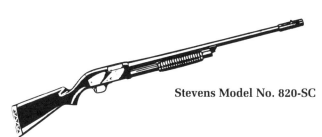

Stevens Model No. 820-SC

**Stevens Model No. 820-SC**
Same as No. 820 except: Savage
"Super Choke"
**Estimated Value: $150.00 - $200.00**

**Stevens Model No. 820**
**Gauge:** 12
**Action:** Slide action; hammerless;
side ejection
**Magazine:** 5-shot tubular
**Barrel:** 28"; improved cylinder,
modified or full choke
**Finish:** Blued; plain walnut semi-
pistol grip stock & grooved slide
handle
**Estimated Value: $140.00 - $175.00**

# Stevens

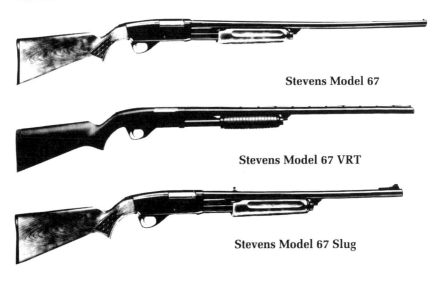

Stevens Model 67

Stevens Model 67 VRT

Stevens Model 67 Slug

## Stevens Models 67 & 67T
**Gauge:** 12, 20, or 410; regular or magnum
**Action:** Slide action; hammerless; side ejecting; repeating
**Magazine:** 4-shot tubular; 3-shot in magnum
**Barrel:** 28" modified or full; 26" full in 410; 30" full in 12 gauge; add 10% for the 67T which has interchangeable choke tubes in 12 & 20 gauge only
**Finish:** Blued; hardwood, semi-pistol grip stock & fluted or grooved slide handle; some with recoil pad
**Estimated Value:** $130.00 - $165.00

## Stevens Models 67 VR & 67 VRT
Similar to the Model 67 except: ventilated rib (67 VR); ventilated rib & interchangeable choke tubes (67 VRT); add 7% for interchangeable choke tubes in 12 or 20 gauge only
**Estimated Value:** $150.00 - $185.00

## Stevens Model 67 Slug
Similar to the Model 67 except: 21" slug barrel & rifle sights; 12 gauge only
**Estimated Value:** $135.00 - $170.00

## Stevens Model 67VRT-K
Similar to the Model 67VR-T except: laminated camo stock; add 8% for interchangable choke tubes
**Estimated Value:** $140.00 - $190.00

## Stevens Model 67T-Y, 67VRT-Y
**Gauge:** 20
**Action:** Slide action; hammerless; repeating
**Magazine:** 4-shot
**Barrel:** 22" with three interchangeable choke tubes; deduct 10% for plain barrel on 67T-Y; ventilated rib on 67VRT-Y
**Finish:** Blued; hardwood, semi-pistol grip stock & grooved slide handle; designed for the young shooter
**Estimated Value:** $140.00 - $175.00

*Pocket Guide to Shotguns*

# Universal

Universal Model 101

**Universal Model 101**
**Gauge:** 12
**Action:** Box lock; top lever, break-open; exposed hammer; single shot
**Magazine:** None
**Barrel:** 28" or 30"; full choke
**Finish:** Blued; plain wood pistol grip stock & tapered forearm
**Estimated Value: $70.00 - $90.00**

**Universal Single Wing**
Similar to the Model 101; made from the early to mid-1970's
**Estimated Value: $75.00 - $95.00**

Universal Model 202

Universal Double Wing

**Universal Double Wing**
Similar to the Model 202 except: 12 or 20 gauge magnum; recoil pad
**Estimated Value: $160.00 - $200.00**

**Universal Model 202**
**Gauge:** 12, 20, or 410; add 10% for 410 ga.
**Action:** Box lock; top lever, break-open; hammerless; double triggers
**Magazine:** None
**Barrel:** Double barrel (side by side); 26" improved cylinder & modified chokes; 28" modified & full chokes
**Finish:** Blued; checkered walnut pistol grip stock & forearm
**Estimated Value: $150.00 - $185.00**

**Universal Model 203**
Similar to the Model 202 except: 10 gauge; 32" full choke barrels
**Estimated Value: $170.00 - $210.00**

**Universal Model 2030**
Similar to the Double Wing except: 10 gauge; 32" full choke barrels
**Estimated Value: $175.00 - $220.00**

# Universal

**Universal Over Wing**

**Universal Auto Wing**

**Universal Duck Wing**

**Universal Over Wing**
**Gauge:** 12 or 20
**Action:** Box lock; top lever, break-open; hammerless; single or double trigger; add 15% for single trigger
**Magazine:** None
**Barrel:** Over & under double barrel; 26", 28", or 30"; ventilated rib
**Finish:** Blued; checkered walnut pistol grip stock & forearm; recoil pad; engraving
**Estimated Value: $300.00 - $375.00**

**Universal Auto Wing**
**Gauge:** 12
**Action:** Semi-automatic
**Magazine:** 5-shot tubular
**Barrel:** 26", 28", or 30"; variety of chokes; ventilated rib
**Finish:** Blued; checkered walnut pistol grip stock & forearm; sights
**Estimated Value: $190.00 - $250.00**

**Universal Duck Wing**
Similar to the Auto Wing except: 28" or 30" full choke; teflon coated barrel
**Estimated Value: $210.00 - $275.00**

# Valmet

Valmet Model 412KE

## Valmet Model 412 KE
**Gauge:** 12
**Action:** Top lever, break-open; hammerless; automatic ejectors
**Magazine:** None
**Barrel:** Over & under double barrel; 26" improved cylinder & modified; 28" modified & full; 30" modified & full in 12 gauge; ventilated rib
**Finish:** Blued; checkered walnut pistol grip stock & forearm; Monte Carlo stock with recoil pad; swivels; interchangeable barrels available to make it a combination shotgun/rifle or a double rifle
**Estimated Value: $420.00 - $560.00**

## Valmet Model 412K
Similar to the Model 412KE except: 36" barrels
**Estimated Value: $420.00 - $560.00**

## Valmet Model 412KE Skeet
Similar to the Model 412KE except: 26" or 28" cylinder bore & improved cylinder bore or skeet choke barrels
**Estimated Value: $480.00 - $600.00**

## Valmet Model 412K Combination
Similar to the Model 412K except: 24" barrels; 12 gauge improved modified barrel over a rifle barrel in caliber 222, 223, 243, 30-06, or 308
**Estimated Value: $470.00 - $625.00**

## Valmet Model 412KE Trap
Similar to the Model 412KE except: 30" improved modified & full choke barrels
**Estimated Value: $480.00 - $600.00**

# Valmet

**Valmet Model 412S**

## Valmet 12 Gauge
**Gauge:** 12
**Action:** Box lock; top lever, break-open; single selective trigger
**Magazine:** None
**Barrel:** Over & under double barrel; 26" improved cylinder & modified; 28" modified & full; 30" modified & full or full & full chokes
**Finish:** Blued; checkered walnut pistol grip stock & wide forearm
**Estimated Value: $320.00 - $425.00**

## Valmet Model 412S
**Gauge:** 12 or 20; regular or magnum
**Action:** Top lever, break-open; hammerless; automatic ejectors; extractor on 36" model
**Magazine:** None
**Barrel:** Over & under double barrel; 26" cylinder bore & improved cylinder, improved cylinder or modified; 28" cylinder bore & modified or modified & full; 30" improved modified & full, modified & full; 36" full; ventilated rib
**Finish:** Blued; checkered walnut pistol grip stock & forearm, adjustable for barrel differences; buttplate adjusts to fit shooter
**Estimated Value: $575.00 - $720.00**

**Valmet Model 412S Combination**

## Valmet Model 412 ST Standard Trap
Similar to the Model 412S except: Monte Carlo stock, 12 gauge only, 30" or 32" barrels; add 30% for Premium Grade Model
**Estimated Value: $690.00 - $860.00**

## Valmet Model 412ST Standard Skeet
Similar to the Model 412S except: 28" skeet choke barrels; add 30% for Premium Grade Model
**Estimated Value: $690.00 - $860.00**

## Valmet Model 412S Combination
Similar to the Model 412S except: 24" barrels; 12 gauge improved modified barrel over a 222, 223, 243, 30-06 or 308 caliber rifle barrel
**Estimated Value: $660.00 - $825.00**

**158**

# Weatherby

## Weatherby Regency
**Gauge:** 12 or 20
**Action:** Box lock; top lever, break-open; hammerless; automatic ejectors; single selective trigger
**Magazine:** None
**Barrel:** Over & under double barrel; 26", 28", or 30"; variety of chokes; ventilated rib
**Finish:** Blued; checkered walnut pistol grip stock & fluted forearm; recoil pad
**Estimated Value: $740.00 - $925.00**

## Weatherby Regency Skeet
Similar to the Regency except: skeet chokes; 26" or 28" barrels
**Estimated Value: $780.00 - $975.00**

## Weatherby Regency Trap
Similar to the Regency except: wide ventilated rib; 30" or 32" full & full, full & improved modified, or full & modified chokes; choice of regular or Monte Carlo stock; 12 gauge only
**Estimated Value: $800.00 - $1,000.00**

Weatherby Olympian

## Weatherby Olympian
**Gauge:** 12 or 20
**Action:** Box lock; top lever, break-open; selective automatic ejectors
**Magazine:** None
**Barrel:** Over & under double barrel; 26" or 28" full & modified; 26" or 28" modified & improved cylinder; 30" full & modified; ventilated rib
**Finish:** Blued; checkered walnut pistol grip stock & fluted forearm; recoil pad
**Estimated Value: $525.00 - $700.00**

## Weatherby Olympian Skeet
Similar to the Olympian except: 26" or 28" skeet choke barrels
**Estimated Value: $620.00 - $775.00**

## Weatherby Olympian Trap
Similar to the Olympian except: ventilated rib on top and between barrels; 30" or 32" barrels; full & modified or full & improved modified chokes; Monte Carlo or regular stock
**Estimated Value: $640.00 - $800.00**

# Weatherby

**Weatherby Orion**

## Weatherby Orion Trap
Similar to the Orion except: 12 gauge only; 30" or 32" full & improved modified or full & modified barrels; wide rib ventilated rib on top and between barrels; Monte Carlo or regular stock
**Estimated Value: $760.00 - $950.00**

## Weatherby Orion Skeet
Similar to the Orion except: 26" skeet choke barrels; 12 or 20 gauge
**Estimated Value: $730.00 - $910.00**

## Weatherby Orion Grade I & Grade III
**Gauge:** 12, 20, 28, or 410
**Action:** Box lock; top lever, break-open; selective automatic ejectors; single selective trigger
**Magazine:** None
**Barrel:** Over & under double barrel; 26" or 28" modified & improved cylinder; 28" or 30" full & modified; ventilated rib; multi-choke after 1983
**Finish:** Blued; checkered walnut pistol grip stock & fluted forearm; rosewood cap at grip; recoil pad; engraved receiver; high-lustre finish; add 28% for Grade III
**Estimated Value: $630.00 - $790.00**

**Weatherby Athena**

## Weatherby Athena Grade IV & Grade V
**Gauge:** 12, 20, 28, or 410
**Action:** Box lock; top lever, break-open; selective automatic ejectors; single selective trigger
**Magazine:** None
**Barrel:** Over & under double barrel; 26" or 28" modified & improved cylinder; 28" modified & full choke; ventilated rib on top & between barrels; multi-choke after 1983
**Finish:** Blued; special selected checkered walnut pistol grip stock & fluted forearm; high-lustre finish; rosewood grip cap; recoil pad; silver gray engraved receiver; add 28% for Grade V
**Estimated Value: $1,175.00 - $1,460.00**

## Weatherby Athena Trap
Similar to the Athena except: 12 gauge only; 30" or 32" full & improved modified or full & modified barrels; wide ventilated rib; with center bead sight; Monte Carlo stock
**Estimated Value: $1,185.00 - $1,480.00**

## Weatherby Athena Skeet
Similar to the Athena except: 26" skeet choke barrels
**Estimated Value: $1,180.00 - $1,470.00**

## Weatherby Athena Single Barrel Trap
Similar quality and workmanship to the Athena Trap; with a single venti-lated rib barrel
**Estimated Value: $1,185.00 - $1,480.00**

**Weatherby Patrician**

**Weatherby Patrician & Patrician II**
**Gauge:** 12; regular (Patrician); 12 magnum (Patrician II)
**Action:** Slide action; hammerless; side ejection
**Magazine:** 2-shot Tubular with plug
**Barrel:** 26", 28", or 30"; variety of chokes; ventilated rib; add 10% for Trap models
**Finish:** Blued; checkered walnut pistol grip stock & grooved slide handle; recoil pad
**Estimated Value: $240.00 - $300.00**

**Weatherby Patrician Deluxe**

**Weatherby Patrician Deluxe**
Similar to the Patrician except: decorated satin silver receiver & higher quality wood
**Estimated Value: $310.00 - $390.00**

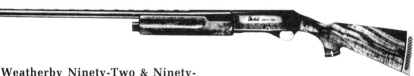

**Weatherby Ninety-Two & Ninety-Two IMC**
**Gauge:** 12; regular or magnum
**Action:** Slide action; hammerless
**Magazine:** 2-shot tubular with plug
**Barrel:** 26" improved cylinder or skeet, 28" modified or full, 30" full; ventilated rib; multi-choke barrel after 1983
**Finish:** Blued; checkered walnut pistol grip stock & slide handle; high-gloss finish; rosewood grip cap; etched receiver; recoil pad
**Estimated Value: $270.00 - $340.00**

**Weatherby Ninety-Two**

**Weatherby Ninety-Two Buckmaster**
Similar to the Ninety-Two except: 22" slug barrel & rifle sights
**Estimated Value: $265.00 - $335.00**

## Weatherby/Western

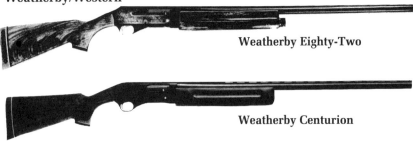

Weatherby Eighty-Two

Weatherby Centurion

### Weatherby Centurion & Centurion II
**Gauge:** 12; regular (Centurion); 12 gauge magnum (Centurion II)
**Action:** Semi-automatic, gas operated; hammerless
**Magazine:** Tubular
**Barrel:** 26", 28", or 30"; variety of chokes; ventilated rib
**Finish:** Blued; checkered walnut pistol grip stock & grooved forearm; recoil pad; add 8% for Trap model
**Estimated Value: $255.00 - $320.00**

### Weatherby Centurion Deluxe
Similar to the Centurion except: decorated satin silver receiver & higher quality wood
**Estimated Value: $285.00 - $360.00**

### Weatherby Eighty-Two & Eighty-Two IMC
**Gauge:** 12; regular or magnum
**Action:** Gas operated, semi-automatic; hammerless
**Magazine:** 2-shot tubular with plug
**Barrel:** 26" improved cylinder or skeet, 28" modified or full, 30" full; ventilated rib; "Multi-Choke" barrel after 1983
**Finish:** Blued; checkered walnut pistol grip stock & forearm; high gloss finish; rosewood grip cap; etched receiver; recoil pad; add 7% for Trap model
**Estimated Value: $330.00 - $415.00**

### Weatherby Eighty-Two Buckmaster
Similar to the Eighty-Two except: 22" slug barrel & rifle sights
**Estimated Value: $330.00 - $415.00**

## Western

### Western Long Range
**Gauge:** 12, 16, 20, or 410
**Action:** Box lock; top lever, break-open; hammerless; double or single trigger; add 10% for single trigger
**Magazine:** None
**Barrel:** Double barrel (side by side); 26" - 32"; modified & full choke
**Finish:** Blued; plain walnut pistol grip stock & forearm
**Estimated Value: $260.00 - $325.00**

Western Long Range

# Western Field

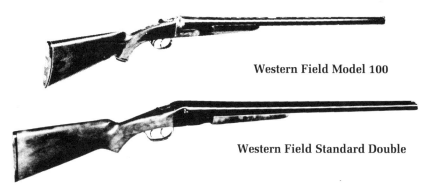

Western Field Model 100

Western Field Standard Double

**Western Field Model 100**
**Gauge:** 12, 16, 20, or 410
**Action:** Box lock; thumb sliding, break-open; hammerless; single shot
**Magazine:** None
**Barrel:** 26"-30"; full choke
**Finish:** Blued; wood semi-pistol grip stock & tapered forearm
**Estimated Value: $60.00 - $75.00**

**Western Field Standard Double**
**Gauge:** 12, 16, 20, or 410
**Action:** Box lock; top lever, break-open; hammerless
**Magazine:** None
**Barrel:** Double barrel (side by side); 26"- 30"; modified & full or full & full chokes; matted rib
**Finish:** Blued; wood semi-pistol grip stock & short tapered forearm
**Estimated Value: $150.00 - $200.00**

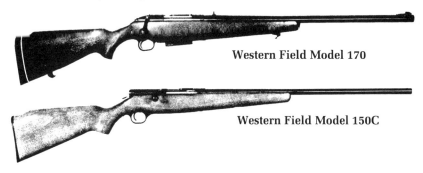

Western Field Model 170

Western Field Model 150C

**Western Field Model 150C**
**Gauge:** 410
**Action:** Bolt action; repeating
**Magazine:** 3-shot; top loading
**Barrel:** 25"; full choke; 3" chamber
**Finish:** Blued; wood Monte Carlo pistol grip one-piece stock & forearm
**Estimated Value: $70.00 - $85.00**

**Western Field Model 170**
**Gauge:** 12
**Action:** Bolt action; repeating
**Magazine:** 3-shot detachable clip
**Barrel:** 28"
**Finish:** Blued; wood Monte Carlo semi-pistol grip one-piece stock & forearm; recoil pad; sights; swivels
**Estimated Value: $70.00 - $90.00**

# Western Field

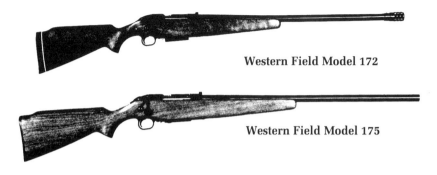

Western Field Model 172

Western Field Model 175

## Western Field Bolt Action
**Gauge:** 12 or 20 (regular or magnum); or 410
**Action:** Bolt action; repeating
**Magazine:** 3-shot detachable box; 410 top loading
**Barrel:** 28"; full choke; 25" in 410
**Finish:** Blued; smooth walnut finish hardwood one-piece pistol grip stock & forearm
**Estimated Value: $75.00 - $90.00**

## Western Field Model 172
Similar to the Model 170 except: without sights or swivels; adjustable choke
**Estimated Value: $65.00 - $80.00**

## Western Field Model 175
Similar to the Model 172 except: 20 gauge; 26" barrel; without adjustable choke
**Estimated Value: $60.00 - $75.00**

Western Field Model 550

## Western Field Model 550 Deluxe
**Gauge:** 12 or 20; regular or magnum
**Action:** Slide action; hammerless; repeating
**Magazine:** 5-shot tubular; 4-shot magnum
**Barrel:** 28" with 3 interchangeable "Accu-Choke" tubes; ventilated rib
**Finish:** Blued; checkered hardwood pistol grip stock & slide handle; chrome damascened finish on bolt; recoil pad; engraved receiver
**Estimated Value: $150.00 - $190.00**

## Western Field Model 550
**Gauge:** 12 or 20 (regular or magnum); and 410 ga.
**Action:** Slide action; hammerless; repeating
**Magazine:** 4-shot magnum, 5-shot regular, tubular
**Barrel:** 26" (410); 30" in 12 or 20 gauge; full or modified choke; add 10% for variable choke; add 10% for optional ventilated rib
**Finish:** Blued; smooth hardwood pistol grip stock with fluted comb; grooved slide handle
**Estimated Value: $140.00 - $175.00**

# Winchester

Winchester Model 20

Winchester Model 37

## Winchester Model 37
**Gauge:** 12, 16, 20, 28, or 410
**Action:** Top lever, break-open; partial exposed hammer; automatic ejector
**Magazine:** None; single shot
**Barrel:** 26"-32"; full or modified choke; or cylinder bore
**Finish:** Blued; plain walnut semi-pistol grip stock & forearm; add $150.00 for 28 gauge; add $25.00 for 410 gauge
**Estimated Value:** $165.00 - $210.00

## Winchester Model 20
**Gauge:** 410
**Action:** Top lever, break-open; exposed hammer
**Magazine:** None; single shot
**Barrel:** 26"; full choke
**Finish:** Blued; plain or checkered wood pistol grip stock & lipped forearm
**Estimated Value:** $190.00 - $250.00

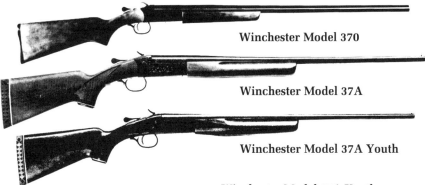

Winchester Model 370

Winchester Model 37A

Winchester Model 37A Youth

## Winchester Model 37A Youth
Similar to the 37A except: 26" barrel & shorter stock
**Estimated Value:** $60.00 - $75.00

## Winchester Model 370
**Gauge:** 12, 16, 20, 28, or 410
**Action:** Top lever, break-open; exposed hammer; single shot; automatic ejector
**Magazine:** None; single shot
**Barrel:** 26"-32" or 36" full choke; modified in 20 gauge
**Finish:** Blued; plain wood semi-pistol grip stock & forearm
**Estimated Value:** $75.00 - $90.00

## Winchester Model 37A
Similar to the Model 370 except: also with 36" Waterfowl barrel; add $5.00 for 36" barrel; checkered stock; fluted forearm; engraved receiver; gold-plated trigger
**Estimated Value:** $65.00 - $85.00

# Winchester

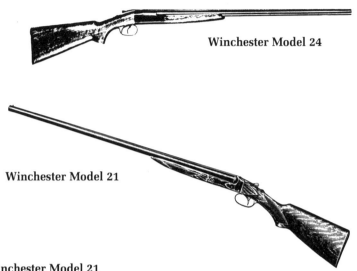

Winchester Model 24

Winchester Model 21

## Winchester Model 21
**Gauge:** 12, 16, or 20
**Action:** Box lock; top lever, break-open; hammerless, double or single trigger
**Magazine:** None
**Barrel:** 26-32" double barrel (side by side); matted or ventilated rib; full, modified or cylinder bore
**Finish:** Checkered walnut, pistol grip stock & forearm
**Estimated Value: $2,000.00 - $2,500.00**

## Winchester Model 24
**Gauge:** 12, 16, or 20
**Action:** Box lock; top lever, break-open; hammerless, automatic ejectors; double triggers
**Magazine:** None
**Barrel:** Double barrel (side by side), 28" cylinder bore & modified in 12 gauge; other gauges modified & full choke; raised matted rib
**Finish:** Blued; plain or checkered walnut pistol grip stock & forearm
**Estimated Value: $265.00 - $350.00**

## Winchester Model 23 Custom
**Gauge:** 12
**Action:** Box lock; top lever, break-open; hammerless, single selective trigger
**Magazine:** None
**Barrel:** Double barrel (side by side), 25½" "Winchoke"
**Finish:** Blued; checkered walnut, pistol grip stock & forearm
**Estimated Value: $1,180.00 - $1,480.00**

## Winchester Model 23 Classic
Similar to the Model 23 Custom except: 26" barrels; 12, 20 or 28 gauge improved cylinder & modified; 410 modified & full choke; engraving on receiver; add 5% for 28 gauge or 410 bore
**Estimated Value: $1,180.00 - $1,480.00**

Winchester Model 23 Pigeon Grade Lightweight

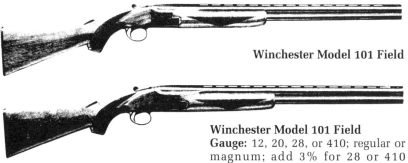

**Winchester Model 23XTR Pigeon Grade**

**Winchester Model 23 Pigeon Grade Lightweight**
Similar to the Model 23 XTR Pigeon Grade except: lighter weight; straight grip stock; rubber butt pad; 25½" barrels
**Estimated Value: $800.00 - $1,065.00**

**Winchester Model 23 XTR Pigeon Grade**
**Gauge:** 12 or 20; regular or magnum
**Action:** Box lock; top lever, break-open; hammerless; selective automatic ejectors; single trigger
**Magazine:** None
**Barrel:** Double barrel (side by side); 26" improved cylinder & modified; 28" modified & full choke; tapered ventilated rib; Winchoke after 1980
**Finish:** Blued; checkered walnut semi-pistol grip stock & forearm; silver gray engraved receiver
**Estimated Value: $820.00 - $1,095.00**

Winchester Model 101 Field

**Winchester Model 101 Skeet**

**Winchester Model 101 Field**
**Gauge:** 12, 20, 28, or 410; regular or magnum; add 3% for 28 or 410 gauge; add $10.00 for magnum
**Action:** Box lock; top lever, break-open; hammerless; single trigger; automatic ejector
**Magazine:** None
**Barrel:** Over & under double barrel; 26"-30"; various choke combinations; ventilated rib
**Finish:** Blued; checkered walnut pistol grip stock & wide forearm; recoil pad on magnum; engraved receiver
**Estimated Value: $700.00 - $940.00**

**Winchester Model 101 Skeet**
Similar to the Model 101 except: skeet stock & chokes; add 3% for 410 or 28 gauge
**Estimated Value: $750.00 - $1,000.00**

# Winchester

Winchester Xpert Model 96

**Winchester Xpert Model 96**
A lower priced version of the Model 101; no engraving; also lacking some of the internal & external extras
Estimated Value: $490.00 - $650.00

**Winchester Model 101 Trap**
Similar to the Model 101 except: regular or Monte Carlo stock; recoil pad; 30" or 32" barrels; 12 gauge only
Estimated Value: $760.00 - $1,020.00

**Winchester Xpert Model 96 Trap**
Similar to the Xpert Model 96 except: Monte Carlo stock; 30" barrel
Estimated Value: $500.00 - $675.00

Winchester Model 101 Lightweight Winchoke

Winchester Model 101 Waterfowl Winchoke

**Winchester Model 101 Waterfowler**
Similar to the Model 101 Waterfowl Winchoke with sandblasted blued finish & low-lustre wood finish
Estimated Value: $940.00 - $1,180.00

**Winchester Model 101 Lightweight Winchoke**
Similar to the Model 101 Field except: interchangeable choke tube system; lighter weight; ventilated rib between barrels as well as on top; 12 or 20 gauge
Estimated Value: $840.00 - $1,050.00

**Winchester Model 101 Waterfowl Winchoke**
Similar to the Model 101 field except: 12 gauge only; 32" barrels; ventilated rib between barrels as well as on top; interchangeable choke tube system; recoil pad
Estimated Value: $690.00 - $920.00

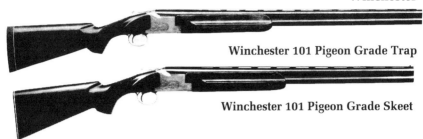

Winchester 101 Pigeon Grade Trap

Winchester 101 Pigeon Grade Skeet

**Winchester 101 Pigeon Grade Skeet**
Similar to the 101 Pigeon Grade except: 27" or 28" skeet choke barrels; front & center sighting beads; also 410 or 28 gauge available
**Estimated Value: $800.00 - $1,000.00**

**Winchester 101 Pigeon Grade Trap**
Similar to the 101 Pigeon Grade except: 30" or 32" barrels; recoil pad; regular or Monte Carlo stock
**Estimated Value: $760.00 - $975.00**

**Winchester 101 Pigeon Grade**
**Gauge:** 12 or 20; regular or magnum
**Action:** Box lock; top lever, break-open; selective automatic ejectors; single selective trigger
**Magazine:** None
**Barrel:** Over & under double barrel; 26" improved cylinder & modified; 28" modified & full; ventilated rib
**Finish:** Blued; checkered walnut pistol grip stock & fluted forearm; silver gray engraved receiver; recoil pad on magnum
**Estimated Value: $720.00 - $900.00**

Winchester Pigeon Grade Featherweight

**Winchester Pigeon Grade Lightweight**
**Gauge:** 12 , 20, or 28
**Action:** Top lever, break-open; hammerless; automatic ejectors; single selective trigger
**Magazine:** None
**Barrel:** Over & under double barrel; 27" or 28" interchangeable choke tubes; ventilated rib on top & between barrels
**Finish:** Blued, silver gray stain finish receiver with etching of gamebirds & scroll work; checkered walnut rounded pistol grip stock & fluted forearm; recoil pad; straight stock available on 28 gauge
**Estimated Value: $1,150.00 - $1,435.00**

**Winchester Pigeon Grade Featherweight**
Similar to the Pigeon Grade Lightweight except: 25½" barrels; improved cylinder & improved modified or improved cylinder & modified; straight grip English style stock; rubber butt pad
**Estimated Value: $890.00 - $1,185.00**

# Winchester

Winchester Diamond Grade Single Barrel

Winchester Diamond Grade O/U Trap

**Winchester Diamond Grade O/U Skeet**
Similar to the Diamond Grade O/U Trap except: 12, 20, 28, or 410 gauge; 27" barrels; add $75.00 for Winchoke
**Estimated Value: $1,150.00 - $1,435.00**

**Winchester Diamond Grade O/U Trap**
**Gauge:** 12
**Action:** Top lever, break-open; hammerless; automatic ejectors; single selective trigger
**Magazine:** None
**Barrel:** Over & under double barrel; 30" or 32" full choke top, inter-changeable choke tube system bottom; ventilated rib on top & between barrels
**Finish:** Blued, silver gray stain finish on receiver with engraving; checkered walnut pistol grip stock & lipped forearm; ebony inlay in pistol grip; regular or Monte Carlo stock; recoil pad
**Estimated Value: $1,115.00 - $1,395.00**

**Winchester Diamond Grade Single Barrel**
Similar in guality and workman ship to the Diamond Grade O/U Trap except: with only one 32" or 34" barrel; interchangeable choke tube system; high-ventilated rib
**Estimated Value: $1,285.00 - $1,610.00**

**Winchester Diamond Grade Combination**
Similar to the Diamond Grade O/U Trap except: with a set of 30" or 32" barrels & a 34" high-rib single barrel; lower barrel & single barrel use interchangeable choke tube system
**Estimated Value: $1,765.00 - $2,200.00**

Winchester Model 501 Grand European Skeet

Winchester Super Grade

**Winchester Super Grade, Shotgun Rifle**
**Gauge:** 12; 3" chamber
**Caliber:** 243 Win., 30-06, 300 Win. mag.
**Action:** Top lever, break-open; hammerless; automatic ejectors; single selective trigger
**Magazine:** None
**Barrel:** Over & under combination; 12 gauge shotgun barrel with interchangeable choke tube system over rifle barrel
**Sights:** Folding leaf rear, blade front
**Finish:** Blued; silver gray satin finish engraved receiver; checkered walnut Monte Carlo pistol grip stock & fluted forearm; recoil pad; swivels. A limited production shotgun/rifle combination
**Estimated Value: $1,435.00 - $1,910.00**

**Winchester Model 501 Grand European Trap**
**Gauge:** 12
**Action:** Top lever, break-open; hammerless; automatic ejectors; single selective trigger
**Magazine:** Nono
**Barrel:** Over & under double barrel; 30" or 32" improved modified & full choke; ventilated rib on top & between barrels
**Finish:** Blued; silver gray satin finish engraved receiver; checkered walnut pistol grip stock & fluted lipped forearm; regular or Monte Carlo stock; recoil pad
**Estimated Value: $975.00 - $1,290.00**

**Winchester Model 501 Grand European Skeet**
Similar to the Model 501 Grand European Trap except: 27" skeet choke barrels; 12 or 20 gauge
**Estimated Value: $975.00 - $1,290.00**

# Winchester

Winchester Model 1901

Winchester Model 36

Winchester Model 41

Winchester Model 97

**Winchester Model 1901**
**Gauge:** 10
**Action:** Lever action; repeating
**Magazine:** 4-shot tubular
**Barrel:** 30" or 32"; full choke
**Finish:** Blued; walnut, pistol grip stock & forearm
**Estimated Value: $560.00 - $700.00**

**Winchester Model 36**
**Gauge:** 9mm shot or ball cartridges
**Action:** Bolt action; single shot; rear cocking piece
**Magazine:** None
**Barrel:** 18"; plain
**Finish:** Blued; straight grip one-piece stock & forearm
**Estimated Value: $220.00 - $275.00**

**Winchester Model 41**
**Gauge:** 410
**Action:** Bolt action; single shot, rear cocking piece
**Magazine:** None
**Barrel:** 24"; full choke
**Finish:** Blued; plain or checkered straight or pistol grip one-piece stock & forearm
**Estimated Value: $200.00 - $250.00**

**Winchester Model 97**
**Gauge:** 12 or 16
**Action:** Slide action; exposed hammer; repeating
**Magazine:** 5-shot tubular
**Barrel:** 26", 28", 30", or 32" modified, full choke or cylinder bore
**Finish:** Blued; plain wood, semi-pistol grip stock & grooved slide handle; made in Field Grade; add $250.00 for Tournament Grade; add $500.00 for Pigeon Grade
**Estimated Value: $360.00 - $450.00**

Winchester Model 97 Trench

Winchester Model 97 Riot Gun

**Winchester Model 97 Riot**
Similar to the Model 97 (field grade)
except: 20" cylinder bore barrel
**Estimated Value: $320.00 - $400.00**

**Winchester Model 97 Trench**
Similar to the 97 Riot Gun with
handguard & bayonet; used in World
War I
**Estimated Value: $480.00 - $600.00**

Winchester Model 12 Pre-'65

**Winchester Model 12**
**Gauge:** 12, 16, 20, or 28
**Action:** Slide action; hammerless;
repeating
**Magazine:** 6-shot tubular
**Barrel:** 26"-32"; standard chokes
**Finish:** Blued; plain or checkered
walnut pistol grip stock & slide
handle; some slide handles grooved;
made in various grades: Standard,
Featherweight, Rib Barrel, Riot Gun,
Duck, Skeet, Trap, Pigeon, Super
Pigeon from 1912 to about 1964; in
1972 Field Gun, Skeet & Trap were
reissued; deduct 50% for guns made
after 1971; priced for Standard
Grade made before 1964; add $50.00
for ventilated rib; $40.00 for raised
matted rib; approximately 50% for
Pigeon & approximately 120% for
Super Pigeon grades; deduct
approximately 25% for Riot Gun
**Estimated Value: $550.00 - $675.00**

**Winchester**

Winchester Model 12 Skeet Pre-'65

Winchester Model 12 Trap Pre-'65

Winchester Model 12 Field After '72

Winchester Model 12 Super Pigeon After '72

Winchester Model 12 Trap After '72

Winchester Model 42

Winchester Model 42 Skeet

**Winchester Model 42**
**Gauge:** 410
**Action:** Slide action; hammerless; repeating
**Magazine:** 5-shot tubular
**Barrel:** 26" or 28"; modified, full choke or cylinder bore
**Finish:** Blued; plain walnut pistol grip stock & grooved slide handle
**Estimated Value: $560.00 - $700.00**

**Winchester Model 42 Skeet**
Similar to the Model 42 except: straight grip stock; matted rib & skeet choke barrel
**Estimated Value: $600.00 - $750.00**

**Winchester Model 42 Deluxe**
Similar to the Model 42 except: higher quality finish; ventilated rib; select wood; checkering
**Estimated Value: $700.00 - $875.00**

Winchester Model 25

Winchester Model 25 Riot Gun

**Winchester Model 25 Riot Gun**
Similar to the Model 25 except: 25" cylinder bore barrel
**Estimated Value: $230.00 - $290.00**

**Winchester Model 25**
**Gauge:** 12
**Action:** Slide action; hammerless; repeating
**Magazine:** 4-shot tubular
**Barrel:** 26" or 28"; improved cylinder, modified or full choke
**Finish:** Blued; plain walnut semi-pistol grip stock & grooved slide handle
**Estimated Value: $270.00 - $340.00**

# Winchester

Winchester Model 1200

## Winchester Model 1200 Field
**Gauge:** 12, 16, or 20; regular or magnum; add $15.00 for magnum
**Action:** Front lock; rotary bolt; slide action; repeating
**Magazine:** 4-shot tubular
**Barrel:** 26"-30"; various chokes or adjustable choke (Winchoke); add $5.00 for adjustable choke; ventilated rib optional; add $25.00 for ventilated rib
**Finish:** Blued; checkered walnut pistol grip stock & slide handle; recoil pad; alloy receiver
**Estimated Value: $175.00 - $220.00**

## Winchester Model 1200 Deer
Similar to the Model 1200 field except: 22" barrel; rifle sights
**Estimated Value: $185.00 - $230.00**

## Winchester Model 1200 Skeet
Similar to 1200 field except: 12 or 20 gauge only; 26" skeet choke barrel; ventilated rib
**Estimated Value: $200.00 - $250.00**

## Winchester Model 1200 Trap
Similar to the 1200 field except: 30" full choke barrel; ventilated rib; regular or Monte Carlo stock
**Estimated Value: $210.00 - $260.00**

Winchester Model 1200 Skeet

## Winchester Model 1200 & 1300 Defender
**Gauge:** 12 or 20; regular or magnum
**Action:** Slide action front lock rotary bolt
**Magazine:** 6-shot tubular; 5-shot in magnum
**Barrel:** 18"; cylinder bore; add 7% for optional rifle sights
**Finish:** Blued; plain wood semi-pistol grip stock & grooved slide handle; a pistol grip model made beginning in 1984
**Estimated Value: $155.00 - $190.00**

## Winchester Model 1200 & 1300 Marine
Same as the Model 1200 Police except: rifle sights
**Estimated Value: $260.00 - $325.00**

## Winchester Model 1200 Police
Same as the Model 1200 Defender except: stainless steel barrel & satin chrome finish on all other external metal parts; also made with shoulder stock or pistol grip (1984); 12 gauge only
**Estimated Value: $230.00 - $290.00**

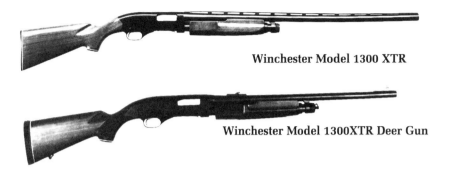

Winchester Model 1300 XTR

Winchester Model 1300XTR Deer Gun

**Winchester Model 1300 XTR**
**Gauge:** 12 or 20; regular or magnum
**Action:** Slide action; hammerless; repeating
**Magazine:** 3-shot tubular
**Barrel:** 26", 28", or 30"; improved cylinder, modified or full choke; ventilated rib optional; add $15.00 for ventilated rib
**Finish:** Blued; checkered walnut pistol grip stock & slide handle
**Estimated Value: $220.00 - $275.00**

**Winchester Model 1300XTR Deer Gun**
Similar to the Model 1300XTR except: 22" slug barrel; rifle sights; sling; recoil pad; 12 gauge only
**Estimated Value: $235.00 - $290.00**

Winchester Model 1300 Winchoke

**Winchester Model 1300 Featherweight**
Similar to the Model 1300 Winchoke except: 22" barrel
**Estimated Value: $215.00 - $270.00**

**Winchester Model 1300 Waterfowl**
Similar to the Model 1300 Featherweight except: sling swivels, 30" barrel; 12 gauge only; dull finish on some models
**Estimated Value: $220.00 - $275.00**

**Winchester Model 1300 Winchoke**
**Gauge:** 12 or 20 magnum
**Action:** Slide action; hammerless; repeating
**Magazine:** 4-shot tubular
**Barrel:** 26"or 28"; ventilated rib; Winchoke system (changeable choke tubes)
**Finish:** Blued; checkered walnut straight or pistol grip stock & slide handle; recoil pad on 12 gauge; Ladies' & Youth Model added 1990
**Estimated Value: $215.00 - $270.00**

## Winchester

**Winchester Model 1300**
**Win-Tuff Deer Gun**
Similar to the Model 1300XTR Deer Gun except: rifled barrel; laminated stock or walnut stock and forearm
**Estimated Value: $255.00 - $320.00**

**Winchester Model 1300 Turkey**
Similar to the Model 1300 Waterfowl except: 22" barrel; add 5% for optional camo finish; add 5% for National Wild, Turkey Federation Model or Ladies' Model
**Estimated Value: $245.00 - $310.00**

**Winchester Ranger**

**Winchester Ranger Deer Gun**

**Winchester Ranger Deer Gun & 1300 Ranger Deer Gun**
Similar to the Ranger except: 22" or 24" cylinder bore deer barrel; rifle sights; recoil pad
**Estimated Value: $180.00 - $225.00**

**Winchester Ranger 1300**
**Deer Combination**
Similar to the Ranger except: 24" cylinder bore deer barrel and interchangeable 28" Winchoke barrel
**Estimated Value: $210.00 - $265.00**

**Winchester Ranger & 1300 Ranger**
**Gauge:** 12 or 20; regular or magnum
**Action:** Slide action; hammerless; side ejecting
**Magazine:** 4-shot tubular; factory installed plug is removable
**Barrel:** 28"; ventilated rib optional; add 15% for vent rib; interchangeable choke tubes
**Finish:** Blued; walnut-finished, semi-pistol grip stock & grooved slide handle; recoil pad
**Estimated Value: $170.00 - $215.00**

**Winchester Ranger Youth, 1300 Ranger Youth**
Similar to the Ranger except: 20 gauge; stock & forearm are modified for young shooters; stock can be replaced with regular size stock; 22" modified or Winchoke barrel
**Estimated Value: $215.00 - $265.00**

**Winchester Model 1911**

**Winchester Model 40**
**Gauge:** 12
**Action:** Semi-automatic; hammerless
**Magazine:** 4-shot tubular
**Barrel:** 28" or 30"; modified or full choke
**Finish:** Blued; plain walnut pistol grip stock & forearm
**Estimated Value: $320.00 - $400.00**

**Winchester Model 1911**
**Gauge:** 12
**Action:** Semi-auto; hammerless
**Magazine:** 4-shot tubular
**Barrel:** 26"-32"; various chokes
**Finish:** Blued; plain or checkered semi-pistol grip stock & forearm
**Estimated Value: $375.00 - $500.00**

**Winchester Model 40 Skeet**
Similar to the Model 40 except: 24" skeet barrel; checkering; "Cutts Compensator"
**Estimated Value: $360.00 - $450.00**

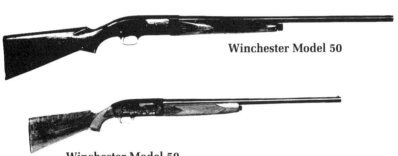

**Winchester Model 50**

**Winchester Model 59**

**Winchester Model 50**
**Gauge:** 12 or 20
**Action:** Semi-automatic; non-recoiling barrel; hammerless
**Magazine:** 2-shot tubular
**Barrel:** 26"-30"; variety of chokes; ventilated rib optional; add $25.00 for ventilated rib
**Finish:** Blued; checkered walnut pistol grip stock & forearm
**Estimated Value: $280.00 - $350.00**

**Winchester Model 50 Trap**
Similar to the Model 50 except: 12 gauge only; Monte Carlo stock; 30" full choke; ventilated rib
**Estimated Value: $335.00 - $420.00**

**Winchester Model 59**
**Gauge:** 12
**Action:** Semi-auto; hammerless; non-recoiling barrel
**Magazine:** 2-shot tubular
**Barrel:** 26"-30"; variety of chokes; steel & glass fiber composition; interchangeable choke tubes optional
**Finish:** Blued; checkered walnut pistol grip stock & forearm; alloy receiver
**Estimated Value: $300.00 - $380.00**

**Winchester Model 50 Skeet**
Similar to the Model 50 except: skeet stock; 26" skeet choke barrel; ventilated rib
**Estimated Value: $335.00 - $420.00**

# Winchester

Winchester Model 1400 Skeet

Winchester Model 1400 Deer

Winchester Model 1400 Mark II

Winchester Model 1400

Winchester Model 1400 Trap

## Winchester Model 1400 & 1400 Winchoke
**Gauge:** 12, 16, or 20
**Action:** Semi-automatic, gas operated
**Magazine:** 2-shot tubular
**Barrel:** 26", 28", or 30"; variety of chokes; adjustable choke after 1978; ventilated rib optional; add $25.00 for ventilated rib
**Finish:** Blued; checkered walnut pistol grip stock & forearm; recoil pad; Cycolak stock with recoil reduction system optional until late 1970's; add $25.00 for Cycolak stock
**Estimated Value: $190.00 - $250.00**

## Winchester Model 1400 Mark II
Similar to the Model 1400 except: lighter weight; with minor improvements
**Estimated Value: $180.00 - $240.00**

## Winchester Model 1400 Deer Gun
Similar to the Model 1400 except: 22" slug barrel; rifle sights
**Estimated Value: $200.00 - $260.00**

## Winchester Model 1400 Skeet
Similar to the Model 1400 except: 12 or 20 gauge; 26" barrel; ventilated rib; add $25.00 for recoil reduction system
**Estimated Value: $210.00 - $280.00**

## Winchester Model 1400 Trap
Similar to the Model 1400 except: 12 gauge; 30" full choke barrel; ventilated rib; regular or Monte Carlo stock; add $25.00 for recoil reduction system
**Estimated Value: $210.00 - $290.00**

Winchester Model 1500 XTR

## Winchester Model 1500 XTR
**Winchoke**
Similar to the Model 1500XTR except: removable choke tube system; 28" barrel only; add $25.00 for ventilated rib
Estimated Value: $240.00 - $320.00

## Winchester Model 1500 XTR
**Gauge:** 12 or 20; regular or magnum
**Action:** Semi-automatic, gas operated
**Magazine:** 3-shot tubular
**Barrel:** 26", 28", or 30"; improved cylinder, modified or full choke; add $25.00 for optional ventilated rib
**Finish:** Blued; checkered walnut pistol grip stock & forearm; alloy receiver
Estimated Value: $225.00 - $300.00

Winchester Ranger 1400 Ranger

## Winchester Ranger Deer & 1400 Ranger Deer
Similar to the 1400 Ranger except: 22" or 24" cylinder bore deer barrel; rifle sights
Estimated Value:  $205.00 - $260.00

## Winchester Ranger & 1400 Ranger
**Gauge:** 12 or 20; regular or magnum
**Action:** Gas operated semi-automatic
**Magazine:** 2-shot
**Barrel:** 26" or 28"; Winchoke interchangeable tubes & ventilated rib
**Finish:** Blued; hardwood semi-pistol grip stock & forearm
Estimated Value: $200.00 - $255.00

## Winchester Ranger Deer Combo
Similar to the 1400 Ranger Deer except: extra 28" ventilated rib Winchoke barrel; hardwood stock
Estimated Value:  $265.00 - $330.00

## Winchester 1400 Slug Hunter
Similar to the 1400 Ranger except: walnut stock and forearm; 22" barrel; improved cylinder and rifled sabot Winchoke tubes; drilled and tapped with scope base and rings; rifle sights
Estimated Value:  $250.00 - $315.00

# Winchester

**Winchester Super X Model I**

**Winchester Super X Model 1 Skeet**
Similar to the Super X Model 1
except: skeet stock; 26" skeet choke
barrel; ventilated rib
**Estimated Value: $300.00 - $400.00**

**Winchester Super X Model 1 Trap**
Similar to the Super X Model 1
except: regular or Monte Carlo stock;
30" full choke barrel; recoil pad
**Estimated Value: $320.00 - $425.00**

**Winchester Super X Model 1 &
Super X Model 1 XTR**
**Gauge:** 12
**Action:** Semi-automatic, gas operated
**Magazine:** 4-shot tubular
**Barrel:** 26"-30"; various chokes;
ventilated rib
**Finish:** Blued; scroll engraved alloy
receiver; checkered walnut pistol
grip stock & forearm
**Estimated Value: $285.00 - $375.00**

# Firearms Glossary

**ACP** - Automatic Colt Pistol. This abbreviation is used to denote ammunition designed for semi-automatic pistols

**Action** - The method by which a firearm is fed ammunition and fired; the portion of the firearm responsible for feeding ammunition, firing, and extracting fired cases

**Adjustable choke** - A muzzle attachment, either factory or manually installed, that allows the shooter to change the choke of his shotgun; several brands are available.

**AE** - Automatic ejector

**Autoloading** - Semi-automatic action; self loading; loads cartridges into chamber using the pressure of a fired cartridge

**Automatic ejector** - A device for extracting the fired case from the chamber when the action is opened

**Automatic safety** - A safety that is put into action by reloading or cocking the fiream

**Barrel** - The part of a gun through which the bullet or shot passes from breech to muzzle

**Barrel adapter** - A device inserted into a barrel to change the gauge or caliber to a smaller size

**Barrel band** - A metal ring encircling the barrel and forearm, found generally on carbines, lever actions, or full length forearms

**Bead** - A type of sight; a small round ball on top of the barrel at the muzzle

**Beavertail** - Wider than average

**Blowback** - A semi-automatic action, this operated by the presssure of the fired cartridge

**Blueing** - A finishing treatment applied to the metal portions of firearms for lasting protection; named for the blue-black final appearance; minimizes light reflection and protects against rust

**Bolt action** - An action, either repeating or single shot, that requires manual operation of the bolt handle to feed the chamber

# Glossary

**Box lock** - An action, with few working parts, found in break-open firearms

**Box magazine** - A box shaped magazine that stores and feeds the cartridges to the chamber

**Breech** - The rear end of the barrel where the chamber is located

**Buck horn** - A type of rear sight; the sides curve upward and inward over the open notch

**Bull barrel** - An unusually thick and heavy barrel

**Butt plate** - A sturdy piece attached to the rearmost section of the stock to protect the wood of the stock

**Buttstock** - The stock; the part of the gun extending from the receiver to the shooter's shoulder

**Caliber** - The diameter of the bore of a rifle or handgun

**Carbine** - A rifle with a short barrel, generally 16" to 20"

**Case-hardened** - A treatment, using carbon and extreme heat, for strengthening metal parts; the treated portion takes on a multi-coloerd, hazy finish

**CB cap** - A 22 caliber cartridge, shorter and less powerful than the 22 caliber short

**CF (Centerfire)** - A cartridge in which the primer is located in the center of the base or head

**Chamber** - The portion of the firearm that holds the cartridge during firing

**Checkering** - Patterned lines cut into the wood of grips, stocks, forearms, and slide handles; it is decorative and, at the same time, provides a non-slip surface.

**Cheekpiece** - An extended area in the stock used for proper cheek positioning against the stock

**Choke** - The design of a shotgun barrel that dictates the spread and pattern of shot leaving the barrel

**Choke tube** - A device that is inserted into the muzzle of a shotgun to alter the choke

**Clip** - A removable magazine, inserted into a firearm, that holds the cartridges and feeds them into the chamber

**Comb** - The upper portion of the stock

**Compensator** - A device attached to the muzzle or made into the barrel to reduce the upward swing of the barrel when fired

**Cylinder** - A rotating cartridge holder used in a revolver, in which the chambers are located

**Damascus barrel** - A type of barrel produced by welding small, twisted pieces of iron and steel in a spiral; these barrels were thought to be stronger in the late 1800's.

**Derringer** - Small, short, one or more barrelled handgun, easily concealed

**Double action (DA)** - Designation of a handgun that can be discharged simply by pulling the trigger; manual cocking is unneccessary

**Double barrel** - A gun with two barrels, lusually a shotgun, rifle, or rifle/shotgun combination with barrels side-by-side or over-and-under

**Double set trigger** - A device with two triggers; one sets a spring mechanism to assist the firing trigger; usually found on target guns

**Dovetail** - A groove by which the sight is attached to the barrel

**Ejector** - A mechanism for removing, or partially removing, empty cases from the gun

**Exposed hammer** - A visible hammer that can be manually cocked

**Extractor** - A device that draws the cartridge or empty case from the chamber when the actin is opened

**Falling block** - An action, found in some early single shots, in which the chamber closing mechanism moves vertically by moving a lever

**Firing Pin** - The device that strikes the primer part of a cartridge to fire the cartridges

**Finish** - The exterior appearance of a gun including type of wood, stock, forearm, and type of metal, sights, decoration, and added features

**Fixed sights** - Stationary sights; not movable

**Flash supressor** - An instsrument that reduces or hides muzzle flame or flash

**Fluted** - A shallow groove or grooves found on some forearms and on revolver cylinders

**Forearm** - The portion of the gun under the barrel that is gripped when firing; usually made of wood; the forearm can be in the form of a slide handle on slide action gun

**Front sight** - The sight at the muzzle end of the barrel

**Gas operation** - A type of action in which gas from a discharging cartridge is used to operate the action

**Gauge** - The bore size of a shotgun

# Glossary

**Grip safety** - A safety device located on the grip of a pistol; the shooter's hand releases the safety as it grips the pistol to fire

**Hammer** - A spring powered piece that strikes the firing pin; it is actuated by the trigger

**Hammerless** - A gun with a concealed hammer or striking mechanism

**Handgun** - A gun that is operated with one hand; revolver, single shot, or semi-automatic pistol

**Handguard** - A piece that fits on top of the barrel to protect the hand from the heat of rapid fire; usually found on military type rifles

**Hooded sight** - A sight with a protective cover

**Lanyard loop or ring** - A metal ring on military handguns that is attached to a strap

**Lever action** - A firearm in which the action is operated by the movement of a lever, usually part of the trigger guard

**Loading gate** - In revolvers a piece that swings open to allow loading; in a long gun, a spring powered door that is forced open when loading cartridges into the magazine

**Long** - The middle designation of a 22 caliber cartridge, longer than a short, shorter than a long rifle

**Long rifle** - The designation of a 22 caliber cartridge; more powerful than a long

**Magazine** - The portion of the gun that holds cartridges ready for feeding into the chamber; in repeating weapons only

**Magnum** - A more powerful cartridge than the standard cartridge of the same caliber

**Mannlicher stock** - A one-piece stock and forearm that extends the length of the barrel

**Micrometer** - A highly accurate adjustable sight found mainly on target rifles or pistols

**Monte Carlo** - A type of stock in which there is a rise at the forward portion; usually has a cheek piece

**Muzzle** - Forward most end of the barrel

**Open sight** - A "notched" sight

**Palm rest** - An adjustable handgrip found on match rifles

**Parkerizing** - A matte, rust resistant surface applied to metal with a phosphate solution; used on military firearms

**Patridge sights** - A square notched rear sight and square post front sight

**Peep sight** - A circular rear sight with a small hole that provides greater accuracy than open or notched sights

**Pistol** - Handgun; usually a semi-automatic handgun

**Pistol grip** - The grip portion of a handgun; or a grip resembling that of a pistol built into the stock of a shotgun or rifle

**Pump** - Slide action

**Ramp sight** - A front sight that is positioned atop a ramp base

**Recoil pad** - A rubber cushion attached to some shotguns and high powered rifles designed to reduce recoil impact on the shooter

**Rem** - Remington

**Repeating** - Any rifle or shotgun that has a magazine and may be fired without reloading after each shot

**Revolver** - A handgun that uses a rotating cylinder to hold and fire cartridges

**Rib** - A flat piece fitted on top of barrel to aid in sighting or add decor; may be ventilated, matte, or solid

**RF (Rimfire)** - A cartridge in which the firing primer is in the perimeter of the shell base or head

**SAA** - Single Action Army

**Safety** - A mechanism that prevents the gun from being fired

**Schnabel** - A decorative lip at the end of a forearm

**Semi-automatic** - An autoloading action in which cartridges are fed automatically; the trigger must be pressed for every desired discharge

**Short** - A small 22 caliber cartridge

**Shotgun** - A non-rifled long gun, designated by gauge, for firing shot shells

**Side lever** - A lever located on the side of a receiver that is tripped to open the gun

**Single action** - The hammer must be cocked before the gun can be fired

**Single set trigger** - A trigger that can be fired by heavy pull or put into another position to allow light pull

# Glossary

**Single trigger** - A single trigger used to fire a double barrel shotgun; a selective single trigger is equipped with a lever that allows the shooter to chose the barrel to be discharged first; the non-selective trigger is always fired in the same, factory-set sequence

**Slide action** - A pump action long arm. An action that requires a manual slide of the forearm section (slide handle) in order to complete the action cycle

**Sling** - A removable strap usually attached to military, high powered hunting and some target rifles or shotguns

**Snubnose** - A revolver with a very short barrel

**Spec. (Special)** - Usually to denote ammunition (as 38 Special)

**S&W** - Smith & Wesson

**Swivel** - A metal loop through which is passed a sling for carrying; either detachable or stationary

**Takedown** - A gun that can be easily taken apart for transport or storage

**TD** - Takedown

**Thumbhole** - A  feature found mostly on match rifles, a hole in the stock for the shooter's thumb

**Thumb lever** - A lever atop the frame that is tripped to break open the firearm

**Thumb rest** - Usually found on handgun grips, a place to rest the thumb to provide better hold

**Trigger** - The piece under the action that is pressed to open the firing mechanism

**Trigger guard** - A metal barrier around the trigger for protection of the trigger

**Tubular magazine** - A tube in which cartridges are stored end to end, ready to be transported to the chamber; can be under barrel or in stock

**UMC** - Union Metallic Cartridge Co.

**Ventilated rib** - A rib that is separated from the barrel by short posts

**Win.** - Winchester

**WMR** - Winchester Magnum Rim Fire

**WRA** - Winchester Repeating Arms Company

# Modern Guns
## Revised Ninth Edition
### by Russell and Steve Quertermous

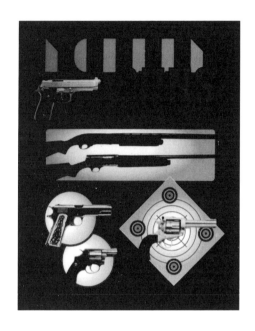

In the 15 years of its existence this book has become a standard reference for gun dealers, hunters, sportsmen and firearms enthusiasts all across the United States. This huge collection features 480 pages crammed full of valuable information and photographs that are indispensable to gun lovers. Over 2,250 models of rifles, handguns and shotguns from 1900 to the present are described and priced in excellent and very good condition with suggested retail prices for those models still in production. More than 1,800 illustrations are included to aid in identification. This popular guide contains model name, gauge or caliber, action, finish on stock and forearm, barrel, cylinder or magazine, sights, weight and length, comments and current market values.

*Modern Guns* is available from your favorite bookseller. If you are unable to find this book in your area, it's available from Collector Books, P.O. Box 3009, Paducah, KY 42002-3009 at $12.95 plus $2.00 for postage and handling.

**8½x11 • 480 Pgs. • PB**                                  **$12.95**

## COLLECTOR BOOKS
*A division of Schroeder Publishing Co., Inc.*

# *New* from the authors of
# MODERN GUNS

Russell and Steve Quertmous have now fine-tuned their speciality and produced a three volume set of handguns, rifles, and shotguns. Therefore, the sportsman collector that limits his field to only one aspect of gun collecting can choose his particular price guide. Each one of these three volumes contains hundreds of illustrations, dates, histories, facts, and current values. It also gives suggested retail values for guns currently still in production. These guides are produced in black and white. The handy 5½x8½ size makes these guides perfect to carry along to shows, auctions, and other gun selling events. So if you are interested in rifles, handguns, or shotguns, now you can choose the book that most interests you.

These books are available from your favorite bookseller or directly from Collector Books, P.O. Box 3009, Paducah, KY 42002-3009 at $9.95 per book plus $2.00 for postage and handling for the first book and 30¢ for each additional book.

**pocket guide to**
# HANDGUNS
**identification & values**
1900 to present

•5½x8½•192 Pgs.
•PB•$9.95

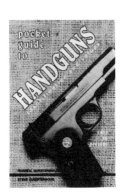

**pocket guide to**
# SHOTGUNS
**identification & values**
1900 to present

•5½x8½•192 Pgs.
•PB•$9.95

**pocket guide to**
# RIFLES
**identification & values**
1900 to present

•5½x8½•192 Pgs.
•PB•$9.95

COLLECTOR BOOKS
*A division of Schroeder Publishing Co., Inc.*

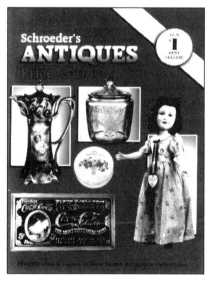